アメリカのレストラン・3
AMERICAN RESTAURANTS III
斎藤 武

アメリカのレストラン・3 AMERICAN RESTAURANTS III
目次 CONTENTS

●Index／索引(都市別／掲載順)　店名／所在地／電話／掲載ページ

はじめに

米国における飲食業界の動きは、最近の2〜3年間をみると
より個性化を前面に打ち出したレストランが多くなってきて
いるようだ。

それは人々のライフスタイルの変化と共に、業態そのものの
変化が要求されるといった背景があるからだ。相変わらず人
気があるのはエスニック・レストランであり、イタリア・メ
キシコ・中国そしてタイやベトナムといった料理の進出が目
覚ましい。多民族、多国籍の人々で構成されるアメリカとい
う超大国の中で種々の影響をお互いに受け、エンジョイする
という環境が生まれるのも自然だし素晴らしい。

「アメリカのレストラン」も3冊目の発行となり、過去70年代
後半から80年代を中心に見てきた米国のレストラン業界も、
本書に収録された32店の中には90年代を目ざした変化の動き
が感じられるものもありそうだ。特にオーナーの考えや姿勢
といったものがより強烈に反映した「ロザリーヌ」「レベッカ」
「カフェイグアナ」、新しい料理方法と美しいプレゼンテーシ
ョンで人気のある「シトラス」や「トミータン」「チャイナ
グリル」、スポーツをテーマにした「ジムマクマホンズ」や
「ハリーカリーズ」などがあり「タンブルウィード」や「ア
メリーク」など女性シェフの活躍も目立ってきた。

本書「アメリカのレストラン・3」に収録されたレストラン
のなかで、いわゆるチェーン店が1・2集ほど目立たないのも、
より個性化を追求する料理や店舗のデザインが要求されてい
る時代を反映しているからであろう。

なお本書は、月刊「飲食店経営」〈㈱商業界発行〉に連載され
たものを中心に、さらに資料などを加えて再編集したもので
店舗の平面プランの作成は1・2集と同じ志田慣平氏に依頼し
ました。

多大な協力を得た関係各位に感謝します。

1989年3月　　　　　　　　　　　　　　　斎藤　武

FOREWORD

A look at the recent American restaurant industry for
the last 2 or 3 years shows an increading number of restaurants that feature more individuality in their design.

It is expected that, along with the new trends in people's
life style, the very styles of business will change. Restaurants that remain popular are those that offer ethnic foods,
such as Italian, Mexican, Chinese, Thai, Vietnamese and
other dishes. In a large country such as the United States,
that include many races and people of different nationali-
ties, people are affected by each other in different ways,
thus creating an enjoyable and wonderful environment.

This book is the third volume of "American Restaurant." Differing from the American restaurant industry
from the latter half of the 1970's to the 1980's, 32 shops
covered by this book seem to include those that are show-
ing signs of changes towards the 1990's. The owner's idea
or policy is intensely reflected in "Rosalie's," "Rebecca's"
and "Cafe Iguana." Restaurants that are popular with new
cooking styles and beautiful presentation are "Citrus,"
"Tommy Tang's" and "China Grill." Restaurants which
adopt sports as a theme include "Jim McMahon's" and
"Harry Caray's." Female chefs are becoming increasing active, and are working in restaurants such as "Tumbleweed"
and "Amérique."

In this "American Restaurant III," the so-called chain
restaurants are less conspicuous than in the first and second
books. This can be explained by the fact that more individualistic dishes and shop designs are being requested
increasingly.

This book is based on a series of articles published in
the monthly magazine "Inshokuten Keiei" (published by
Shogyokai Co., Ltd.) which were reedited with the addition
of supplementary data. As in the case of the first and
second books, I asked Mr. Kanpei Shida for cooperation in
preparation of shop plans.

Many thanks go to people concerned who have kindly
extended cooperation.

March 1989

Gen Takeshi Saito

Published by **Shotenkenchiku-sha Co., Ltd.**
7-22-36-2, Nishi-shinjuku, Shinjuku-ku,
Tokyo 160 Japan

別冊商店建築42 アメリカのレストラン・3 1989年3月31日発行

著者　斎藤　武　　　　　編集●辻田　博　　　　協力スタッフ
編集発行人　村上末吉　　制作●菅谷良夫　　　　表紙デザイン●ウィークエンド　　　　印刷●小堀製版印刷
　　　　　　　　　　　　　　　　　　　　　　　本文レイアウト●ぱとおく社　　　　　写植●福島写植
　　　　　　　　　　　　　　　　　　　　　　　英文●海広社　　　　　　　　　　　　製本●坂田製本／山田製本

発行所　株式会社商店建築Ⓒ
　　　　本社　東京都新宿区西新宿7-22-36-2 〒160 TEL(03)363-5770代
　　　　支社　大阪市中央区西心斎橋1-9-28第3大京ビル 〒542 TEL(06)251-6523代
ISBN 4-7858-0003-8

段差のあるハイテク感覚のダイニングエリアと奥にオープンキッチンとテラスをみる
The high tech sense dining area featuring different levels, and the inner open kitchen and terrace.

Bistango

19100 Von Karman Ave. Irvine, CA 92715 Phone/714-752-5222

新しいオフィスビル「THE ATRIUM」の外観と　その1階にあるレストラン
The appearance of the new office building "The Atrium" and the restaurant at the 1st floor.

店内左奥のコーナーの入口あたりよりモダン感覚のダイニングルームをみる
The modern sense dining room viewed from the entrance at an inner left corner.

ローカルのアーチストによる絵画の壁面構成は定期的に替えられ　ギャラリーの雰囲気をもたせて好評

自然光の入る窓際には竹を導入している

Top / The composition of pictures on the wall painted by local artists, is periodically changed, giving a gallery-like atmosphere that is favorably accepted.

Bottom / Bamboos are introduced into an area by the window from which natural light comes in.

カクタスがある店内中央部の開放的なテーブル席をみる

The open table seats in the center which features cactuses.

ビスタンゴ

この店は　ビバリーヒルズにある本店の2号店で　南カリフォルニアのアーバインにある近代的なオフィスビルの1階に　1987年11月に開店した。年々発展を続けるアーバイン市への出店は本店の知名度とともに話題を呼んでいる。

店名はビストロとタンゴを合わせた造語である。料理はイタリア料理風のものを中心に日本人の副料理長を加えて　日本的なフランス料理を盛り込むなど新しいスタイルを生み出している。

モダンなハイテク感覚のインテリアはロンドン出身の建築家　Michael Carapetianが手がけ　ダイニングエリアはマルチプルに変化をつけて広がりを充分に生かしている。オープンキッチンを設けて調理場の動きを見せたり　車付きの円形ワインカートを採用して　自慢のワインのグラス売りの販促に役立てるなど　本店とは異なるコンセプトを生み出している。

開店／1987年11月14日
営業時間／11:15AM～3:00PM(ランチ：月～金)
　　　　　5:30PM～12:00AM(ディナー：月～土)
　　　　　4:30PM～11:00PM(ディナーのみ：日)
客席数／180席(レストラン) 70席(バー)　従業員数／75人
客単価／ランチ 10～12ドル　ディナー 15ドル

8

BISTANGO

This is the second shop for the owner whose main shop is located in Beverly Hills, and opened in November 1987 at the 1st floor of a modern office building in Irvine, South California. The opening of this shop in Irvine City, a town in continuous development, is drawing much attention, associated with the popularity of the main shop.

The shop name is a coinage combining bistro and tango. Along with main Italian dishes, they also serve new-style dishes, such as French dishes cooked by an assistant Japanese chef employing Japanese elements.

The modern interior with a high tech sense has been undertaken by Michael Carapetian, an architect from London. The dining area features a multiple variation to fully utilize the expansive space. The open kitchen allows guests to observe operations in the cooking room, and a round wheeled wine-cart is used to cater wine that is the pride of this shop. Thus, this shop differentiates itself in concept from the main shop.

Design / Michael Carapetian　　Management / John Choukassian
Opened / November 14, 1987
Open / 11:15 a.m. to 3:00 p.m. (lunch: Mon. to Fri.),
　　　　5:30 p.m. to 12:00 a.m. (dinner: Mon. to Sat.)
　　　　4:30 p.m. to 11:00 p.m. (dinner alone: Sun.)
No. of guest seats / 180 (restaurant), 70 (bar)
No. of employees / 75
Price per guest / lunch: $10 to $12, dinner: $15

店内中央の一段高いテーブル席は車椅子でも利用できるようにスロープで結ばれている
The table seats in the center are a little higher than the surrounding areas, and connected with a slope so that they may also be utilized by wheelchair users.

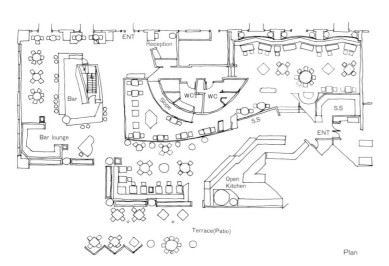

Plan

入口近くに設けられた車椅子用の通路
The aisle for wheelchairs provided near the entrance.

ワインは200種以上も揃え　ハードリッカーも飲めるバーコーナー

円形のワイン用サービスワゴンは移動が可能で　ワインのグラス売りの販促に役立てている

Top / Provided with more than 200 types of wine, this bar corner can also serve hard liquor.

Bottom / Since the round wagon for wine service is movable, it is helping sales promotion of wine in glass service.

店内中央部よりバーコーナーをみる　ユニークな形の赤いワインセラーが印象的
The bar corner viewed from the shop's center. The uniquely shaped red wine cellar is impressive.

日本製の真赤なスツールを配したバーコーナー　カウンタートップはブラジル製の大理石
The bar corner accented with deep red stools of Japanese make. The counter top is finished with Brazilian marble.

①

②

③

④

1／寿司を思わせる鮪のタルタル　アボガド　パパイヤ　ラディッシオとアンディーブ添え

2／仔牛と牛のカルパッシオ　アルコラとケイハー　パルメザンチーズ添え

3／カニのコロッケと市場のレタス　ピンクグレープフルーツのソース

4／ホタテ貝のナポレオン　ホーレン草　ザリガニ添えシャンペンバターソース

1/ Hai tuna tartar with avocado, papaya, radicchio and endive.
2/ Carpaccio of veal and beef with arrugola capers and parmesan.
3/ Sauteed crab cake with mache lettuce and pink grapefruit sauce.
4/ Napoleon of sea scallops, spinach and cray fish with champagne butter.

PAZZIA

755 N. La Cienega Blvd. Los Angeles, CA 90069
Phone/213-657-9271

パッツィア
スタイリッシュで一味変わったイタリア料理店（トラットリア）が"ディナーハウス通り"といわれるラ シエネガ通りに新しく加わり話題となっている。「パッツィア」は最も美しく ソフィスティケイトされたアメリカのイタリア料理店として有名なロサンゼルスのダウンタウンの「Rex il Ristorante」の姉妹店としてオープンした。オーナーの Mauro Vincenti 氏は 元映画制作者であっただけに 店舗づくりから食器 テーブルセッティング 料理 サービスにいたるまで 完全主義者としてこの店づくりにも気を配っている。店名は"気違いじみた"（クレイジー）という意味のイタリア語で 開店までに3年という期間がかかり 設計家さがし 難工事 周辺住民との話し合いなど 多くの問題をかかえた上での難産だったことから 名付けたという。新生なったこのコンテンポラリィなイタリア料理店は本店に比べて約半額という客単価であり イタリアから迎えたシェフ Bombana Umberto の美しいモダンイタリア料理が味わえる店である。
開店／1988年4月16日
営業時間／12：00PM～2：30PM（ランチ）
　　　　　　6：30PM～10：30PM（ディナー）
休日／日曜日
客席数／86席（レストラン）40席（パティオ）24席（ティールーム）
従業員数／38人（内キッチン18人）
客単価／ランチ 22ドル　ディナー 35ドル

PAZZIA

"Trattoria," a stylish and queer Italian restaurant, joined Cienega Blvd that is dubbed the "Dinner House Street," drawing hot attention. "Pazzia" opened as a sister" shop of Rex il Ristorante" at downtown Los Angeles, that is famous as the most beautiful sophisticated Italian restaurant in America. The owner, Mr. Mauro Vincenti, was formerly a movie film producer so that, as a perfectionist, he is very particular about every arrangement, from tableware to table setting, dishes and services.
The shop name is an Italian meaning "crazy." It was chosen since it has taken three years till opening, and had a difficult delivery with many problems, such as difficulty in finding an adequate designer, difficult construction, and negotiations with the neighboring inhabitants.
The newly born contemporary Italian restaurant serves dishes at unit prices per guest half the one offered at the main shop. Here, modern beautiful Italian dishes cooked by Bombana Umberto, the chef from Italy, can be enjoyed.

Opened / April 16, 1988
Open / 12:00 p.m. to 2:30 p.m. (lunch),
　　　　6:30 p.m. to 10:30 p.m. (dinner)
Closed / Sunday
No. of guest seats / 86 (restaurant), 40 (patio),
　　　　　　　　　24 (tea room)
No. of employees / 38 (18 at kitchen)
Price per guest / lunch: $22, dinner: $35

ゆるやかなスロープと人工池を設けたレストランへのアプローチ
The approach to the restaurant provided with a gentle slope and pool.

新進デザイナー Craig Jenkins が担当したロゴがテラスの入口にみえる
The logo designed by Craig Jenkins, a rising designer, is visible at the entrance of the terrace.

南カリフォルニアの開放的なテラス空間を中央に設けて　その左右にレストランとティールームが展開する
The restaurant and tea room open in both sides of South Californian open terrace space.

スロープを登りきったあたりよりレストランの入口をみる
The entrance of the restaurant viewed from atop the slope.

スタイリッシュなデザインコンセプトを導入した入口の演出　予約受付の
専任者を置いている
The entrance presentation introducing a stylish design concept.
With a full-time reservation receptionist.

ハイテク感覚の店舗は手前よりダイニングルーム　中央にテラス　その向うにティールームと３つの異なる空間で構成している
The inside space of the high tech sense restaurant is composed of three different segments — dining room in your side, terrace in the center and tea room behind.

コーナーに設けられた螺旋階段は2階トイレへ通じる　壁面の絵はイタリア人の作品

階段上よりみるテーブル席と左奥がレストランの入口

Top / The spiral staircase at the corner leads to the 2nd floor toilet. Pictures on the wall are pieces painted by an Italian.
Bottom / The table seat area viewed from atop the staircase; visible at an inner left part is the entrance of the restaurant.

上　下／イタリアのトラットリア（Trattoria＝飲食店）を演出した86席のダイニングルーム

Top, bottom / The 86-seat dining room presenting an image of Italian trattoria (restaurant).

天井空間も高く　壁面から家具　調度品　器に至るまでトータルな完成度を求めるオーナーの姿勢が反映しているレストラン
The high ceiling, wall, furniture and utensils, and tableware—all these interior elements of this restaurant reflect the owner's pursuit of total perfection.

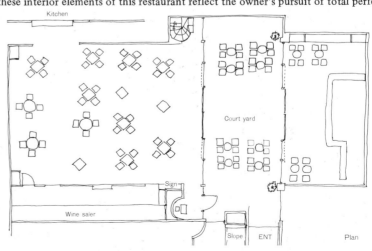

壁面内に広いワインセラーを設け　ヨーロッパやカリフォルニア産のワインのコレクションが自慢の店
This restaurant features a wide wine cellar in the wall where a collection of European, Californian and other wine is stored.

ダイニングルームの右奥に設けているオープンキッチン　円形テーブルの下方の大理石やモダンアートはイタリアより導入したもの
The open kitchen at an inner right part of the dining room. The marble beneath the round table, modern art, etc. have been introduced from Italy.

左／イタリアから迎えたシ
　ェフ Bombana Umberto
　のモダンイタリア料理
　も好評
右／カルパッシオ（Carpaccio）
　と海老のオードブル
　フレッシュフルーツ添
　え

Left / Modern Italian dishes served by Bombana Umberto, chef from Italy, are favorably accepted.
Right / Hors d'œuvre of carpaccio and shrimps, with fresh fruits.

上　右下／24席のティールーム　ジェラートやカプチーノのマシンはイタリア製
Top, bottom right / The 24-seat tea room.　Galato and cappucino machines are of Italian make.

自家製デザートの盛合せ 7.50ドル　三色のジェラート 4.50ドル
Assorted homemade dessert — tricolor gelato.

パームツリーに囲まれたショッピングセンター内のレストランの核として出店したブラッセリー
A brasserie opened as the main restaurant within the shopping center surrounded with palm trees.

Langan's Brasserie

10250 Santa Monica Blvd. Los Angeles, CA. 90067　Phone/213-785-0961

The entrance to the brasserie opening from morning till nearly midnight. Visible in the right side is a seafood showcase.

朝から夜中近くまで営業しているブラッセリーの入口　右側に見える
のがシーフードのショーケース

レセプションよりダイニングエリアをみる
The dining area viewed from the reception.

ダイニングエリアよりバー方向をみる　　The bar corner adjacent to the dining area.

ランガンス ブラッセリー

ロンドンに本店を持つ「ランガンズ ブラッセリー」が
センチュリーシティにあるショッピングセンター内に出
店し 新しいコンセプトの一つの大きな核として話題と
なっている。イギリスの植民地であるバハマの雰囲気を
持つ11,000平方フィートの店内には オリジナルの水彩
画や油絵が飾られ20m以上もある長いチェリーウッドの
バーカウンターを設けている。また新鮮な牡蠣やシュリ
ンプ 蟹などをサービスするシーフードバーを設けてい
るのも特徴。提供する料理はオーナーとシェフよりすぐ
りのバラエティのあるアイテムばかり。中にはイギリス
人たちの好むフィッシュ & チップスを加えることも忘
れていない。
ブラッセリーというサービス形態は アイドルタイムの
ない終日開店（オールタイム営業）ということから 朝
食メニューにはじまり ランチメニュー その後に続く
限定したスモールメニュー ディナーメニューとバーメ
ニューにより構成されている。
開店／1988年6月3日
営業時間／ 7:30AM〜11:30AM（朝食）
　　　　　 11:30AM〜 3:00PM（ランチ）
　　　　　 3:00PM〜 6:00PM（ティータイム
　　　　　 & スモールメニュー）
　　　　　 6:00PM〜11:00PM（ディナー）
　　　　　 2:00AMまで（バー）
客席数／180席（ダイニングエリア）
　　　　 130席（バーエリア）
従業員数／120人
客単価／ランチ10〜12ドル　ディナー12〜15ドル

LANGAN'S BRASSERIE

"Langan's Brasserie" whose main shop is in London,
opened its branch shop in a shopping center in Century
City, drawing attention of the public for its new concept. In the 11,000 sq. feet shop with an atmosphere
of Bahama, colony of the U.K., are displayed original
water color paintings and oil paintings, and a cherry
wood bar counter longer than 20 cm is provided.
Another feature is a seafood bar serving fresh oyster,
shrimps, crab, etc. All the dishes are the choicest
varieties recommended by the owner and chef. Fish
and chips preferred by English people are also offered.
Since the brasserie service style features an all-time
operation, its menu starts from breakfast to lunch,
followed by small, dinner and bar menu.

Opened / June 3, 1988
Open /　7:30 a.m. to 11:30 a.m. (breakfast)
　　　　 11:30 a.m. to 3:00 p.m. (lunch)
　　　　 3:00 p.m. to 6:00 p.m.
　　　　　 (teatime & small menu)
　　　　 6:00 p.m. to 11:00 p.m. (dinner)
　　　　 Up to 2:00 a.m. (bar)
No. of guest seats /　186 (dining area)
　　　　　　　　　　 130 (bar area)
No. of employees /　120
Price per guest / lunch: $10 to 12,　dinner: $12 to 15

ダイニングエリア中央部より長いバーカウンター部をみる

The long bar counter section viewed from the center of the dining area.

この広いテーブル席とその奥の小さな部屋にはオリジナルの絵画が飾ってある（180席）
Original pictures are displayed in this wide table seat area and the small room behind.

広いダイニングエリアの奥より入口方向をみる
The entrance area viewed from an inner part of the wide dining area.

バハマの雰囲気を演出している明るいダイニングエリアはピカピカに磨かれた木製フロア
The bright dining area having a Bahamian atmosphere features the wooden floor that is given a good shine.

バハマ風のデコアと絵画が飾られたダイニングエリア
The dining area coming with a Bahamian decor and pictures.

上・左下／70フィート（約20ｍ）の長いバーカウンターではシャンペンやワインのほかにスペシャルドリンクスのオリジナルカクテルも用意されている
Top, bottom / The long (about 70 feet) bar counter serves champagne, wine, and original cocktails as special drinks.

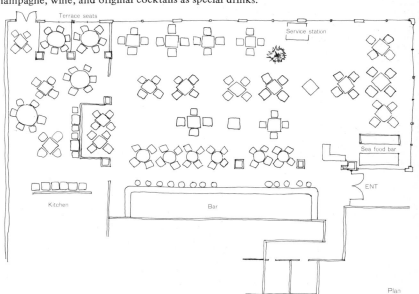

ダイニングエリアに隣接したバーコーナーをみる

The bar corner viewed from the dining

ダイニングエリアに立つシェフの Jonathan Parker 氏　Jonathan Parker, chef, standing at the dining area.

①

②

③

主な料理

1/ Langan's fish and chips.
2/ Fruit steeped in spice.
3/ Guinea hen with tart crabapple charlott.

レセプション近くにあるシーフードバー　シャンペンと共に新鮮な魚介類を味わえる
The seafood bar near the reception, serves champagne and fresh fish and shellfish dishes.

ガラス張りのサイドウォークカフェを設けたファサード The facade provided with a glassed sidewalk cafe.

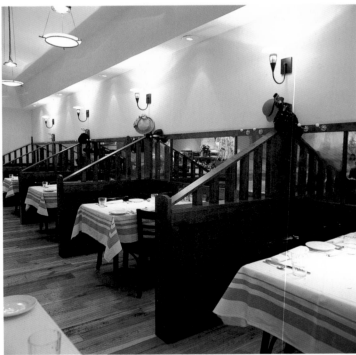

コンテンポラリーな照明のブース席コーナー
The booth seat corner featuring contemporary lighting.

Bistro 110

110 East Pearson St. Chicago, Illinois 60611
Phone/312-266-3110

ブース席とダイニングエリアを段差で分けている　　　　　　　　　The booth seat and dining areas segmented by a difference in level.

有名な画家Judy Rifka氏による壁画が店内をうめている　　The pictures painted by Mr. Judy Rifka, a well-known painter, fill up the inside.

1/ポートワインとコニャックでマリネしたニューヨークダックのレバーのテリーヌ　2/ガーリック　ローズマリー　タイムを加えたマッシュルームのロースト　3/当店のスペシャリティ　チキンのロースト

1/ Fresh foie gras　　2/ Woodburning oven roasted mushrooms　　3/ Half chicken

メニューの50〜60%はローストによる調理法で料理を提供するオープンキッチン
50 to 60% of menu items consist of dishes cooked by means of roasting at this open kitchen.

カラフルな壁画と松材のフロアに温かい照明のダイニングエリア
The warm-lighted dining area featuring colorful wall painting and pinewood floor.

ビストロ 110

シカゴのウォータータワープレイスは　旅行者たちが多く訪れる所として有名だが　その一角にあるカジュアルで　ヨーロッパの伝統的なビストロを想わせるレストランである。元は地元で有名なレストラン　「Brackhawk on Pearson」だった場所だ。シカゴで24店のレストランを経営する「The Levy Organization」の　Larry and Mark Levy と「ブラック フォーク」の経営者の息子 Dong Roth が共同で経営するこの新しいコンセプトのビストロは 195の客席を3つのエリアに分け　ガラス張りのサイドウォーク カフェとコンテンポラリィな照明　アーティストの Judy Rifka による壁画　松材のフロア　木を燃やすオーブンを備えたオープンキッチンなどで構成している。調理はその50〜60%がローストによる方法でガーリックやタイム　種々のハーブ類の香りを強調した料理が多いのも特徴だ。

開店／1987年10月
営業時間／11:30AM〜11:00PM（月〜木）
　　　　　11:30AM〜12:00AM（金・土）
　　　　　4:00PM〜10:00PM（日）
客席数／195席
客単価／ランチ12〜15ドル　ディナー18〜20ドル

BISTRO 110

Water Tower Place in Chicago is famous as a place frequented by tourists. "Bistro 110" open at a corner of this place, is a casual restaurant reminding us of a traditional European bistro. Formerly occupied by "Brackhawk on Pearson," it is patronized by local people. This new-concept bistro jointly managed by Larry and Mark Levy of "The Levy Organization" who run 24 restaurants in Chicago, and Dong Roth, son of the manager of "Blackhawk," is equipped with 195 guest seats that are partitioned into three areas. The interior consists of glassed sidewalks, cafe, contemporary lighting, fresco painted by the artist Judy Rifka, pine floor, open kitchen with a wood burning oven, etc. 50 to 60% of cooking is made on roasting. Many dishes are flavored with garlic, thyme, and various kinds of herbs.

Opened / October 1987
Open / 11:30 a.m. to 11:00 p.m.
　　　　　(Monday to Thursday)
　　　　　11:30 a.m. to 12:00 a.m.
　　　　　(Friday · Saturday)
　　　　　4:00 p.m. to 10:00 p.m. (Sunday)
No. of guest seats / 195
Price per guest / lunch: $12 to 15, dinner: $18 to 20

レストラン後方のオープンキッチン

The open kitchen behind the restaurant.

入口近くのレセプションとブース席コーナー

The reception near the entrance and booth seat corner.

バーとメインダイニングの間に設けられたテーブルトップ用のペーパーロールのあるサービス台

Service table with tabletop paper rolls provided between the bar and main dining areas.

サイドウォークカフェのダイニングエリアとバーコーナー   The dining area and bar corner of the sidewalk cafe.

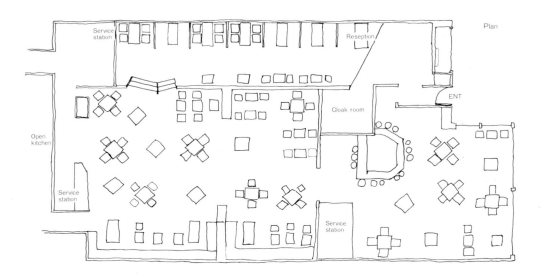

ファサード　元印刷所のロフトスペースを改装したもの
The facade.　The redecorated loft space of a former printing house.

大きな円柱を配した入口近くのレセプションあたり
The reception area near the entrance where large columns are arranged.

AMÉRIQUE

900 N. Franklin St. Chicago, Illinois 60610
Phone/312-943-6341

店内の奥行いっぱいに走るダクトの下にハイテク感覚のバーエリアと後方にダイニングエリア
The high tech sense bar area and dining area under the ducts that fully run along the depth.

エントランス　大きなガラス面にマスコミの紹介記事を飾っている

入口のドアを開けるとバーがあり　その後方には手作り人形がカラフルに並んでいる

Left, top / The entrance. The large glass surface decorated with articles appeared on newspapers, etc.

Left, bottom / You see this bar when opening the entrance door, and at an inner part are handmade dolls arranged colorfully.

Right, top / The bar counter with 15 seats features a U-shaped high tech sense, where guests can enjoy a "happy hour."

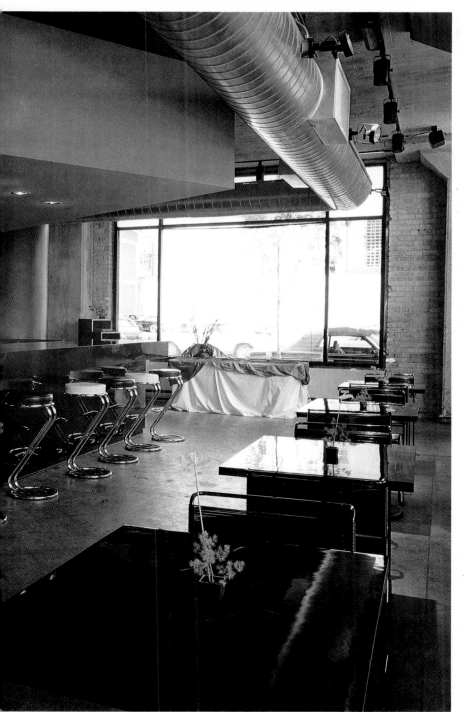

アメリーク

シカゴ川の流れる北の一角 リバーノースにある倉庫街が再開発され オフィスやギャラリー レストランなどの進出で注目されている。「アメリーク」は元印刷所のロフトスペースの1階を改装したもので 若い女性オーナーシェフが中心になってユニークなインテリアと料理を生みだしている。

倉庫の雰囲気を生かし 煉瓦の壁やコンクリートの床やアルミのダクトなどうまくインテリアとして利用しており リラックスな雰囲気というよりはむしろハイテク感覚のよりアップビートといった感じだ。

料理はフランス料理と現代的な料理をミックスしたエクレクティックなもので 新しい料理の開発がみられ シーズンごとに変えるメニューには 野菜やつけ合わせ ソースなどに幅広い変化をつけている。オーナーのジェニファー ニューベリィ(Jennifer Newbury)さんはシカゴやロサンゼルスの数多くのレストランで働き その経験を生かしているが 最近 新しいシェフを迎え2人のシェフによるメニュー開発に力を入れている。

開店／1985年9月1日
営業時間／12:00PM～ 2:15PM(ランチ：火～金)
　　　　　　6:00PM～10:00PM(ディナー：火～土)
休日／日曜日
客席数／75席(レストラン)　15席(バーエリア)
従業員数／25人
客単価／ランチ14ドル　ディナー25ドル(フードのみ)

AMÉRIQUE

A warehouse street at River North, a northern corner where River Chicago is running, has been redeveloped, and it draws much attention since offices, galleries, restaurants, etc. have chosen this street. "Amérique" came into being by redecorating the 1st floor loft space of a former printing house. The young female owner-chef was the main responsible for the interior design, and is serving unique dishes.

To emphasize the warehouse's atmosphere, the brick wall, concrete floor, aluminum duct, etc. are incorporated skillfully into the interior. Rather than a relaxed atmosphere, it gives a high tech, up-beat sense.

The dishes are eclectic mixing French with modern dishes. By developing new dishes, the menu is changed from season to season, accompanied by a variety of vegetables, garnish sauce, etc. The owner, Jennifer Newbury, worked in many restaurants in Chicago, Los Angeles, etc., and she uses fully her experience in the restaurant operation. Recently, she has employed a new chef, and these two chefs are endeavoring to develop a new menu.

Opened / September 1, 1985
Open /　12:00 p.m. to 2:15 p.m.
　　　　　　(lunch: Tuesday to Friday)
　　　　　6:00 p.m. to 10:00 p.m.
　　　　　　(dinner: Tuesday · Saturday)
Closed / Sunday
No. of guest seats / 75 (restaurant), 15 (bar area)
No. of employees / 25
Price per guest / lunch: $14, dinner: $25 (food only)

15席のバーカウンターはU字型のハイテク感覚　ハッピーアワーもある

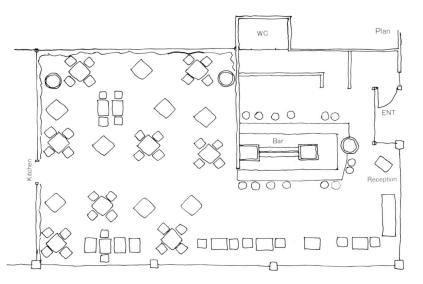

①

②

③

④

1／ガーリックのベイク（山羊のチーズ添えと 5 種類のプチサラダ）
2／サーモングリル（ウォータークレス ソース）
3／仔牛のパン粉包み 羊乳チーズ焼き デミグラソースかけ
4／洋梨のタルト　クリームとカラメルソース

The main dishes.

左／フラワーデザイナーが定期的に模様変えをする布の壁面デザイン

Left / The cloth wall design changed periodically by a flower designer.

ダイニングエリアは布地で構成する壁面とそのバックライトのカラフルさがアップビートな雰囲気を醸し出す
The dining area, with the cloth surface wall and its colorful back light, produces an up-beat atmosphere.

コンクリートの床　レンガの壁面　長いダクトなど　元印刷所にあったものをそのまま生かしている
The concrete floor, bricked wall, long ducts, etc. — those that existed at the former printing house are used as they are.

若手のオーナーシェフ（女性）を中心に若いクルーたちが働く
Young crew working under the leadership of the young owner-chef (woman).

店内がよく見えるオープンな雰囲気をもったファサードはビバリードライブ通りに面している
Having an open atmosphere that allows you to look into the inside well, the facade faces Beverly Drive Street.

テーブル席中央部にある農家をイメージした Jane Krensky 氏のアート作品
Jane Krensky's pieces of art in the center of the table seat area that gives an image of farmhouse.

T U M B L E W E E D

130 South Beverly Drive Beverly Hills, CA 90212
Phone/213-274-5844

錫製のランタンやブッチャーペーパーがテーブル席を構成するカジュアルな雰囲気のレストラン
The restaurant having a casual atmosphere with tin lanterns and butcher paper accenting the table seat area.

タンブルウィード

テキサス生まれの若き女性シェフが経営し　新しいスタイルの南部料理を提供す
るカジュアルな雰囲気のレストランである。シェフのギルモア（Elka Gilmore）さ
んは"自分の料理は毎日でも食べたい料理である"といい　特にテキサスでよく親
しまれているバーベキューや炭焼きでスモークした調理法に彼女独自のソースを
加えて特色を出している。
1987年度の全米シーフード料理コンテスト（American Seafood Challenge）で 2
位　1988年度のカリフォルニア　シーフード　チャレンジではグランプリを得て
全米コンテストへの参加権を手にするなど注目されている。
最近　アメリカでは女性のシェフ希望者が多く　彼女もその成功者の一人として
全米に認められた存在となった。店内の黄色い壁面に飾った田舎の風景写真は
ハンドメイドで着色した Jane Krensky の作品であり　ギルモア　シェフの料理と
共にアーティスティックな雰囲気を演出している。
開店／1987年12月1日
営業時間／11：30AM～ 2：30PM（ランチ：月～金）
　　　　　6：00PM～10：30PM（ディナー：日～木）
　　　　　6：00PM～11：30PM（ディナー：金・土）
客席数／46席
客単価／アントレ 8 ～19ドル　料理50～70ドル（ 2 人）

TUMBLEWEED

Managed by a young female chef born in Texas, "Tumbleweed" is a casual
restaurant serving southern dishes in new styles. Commenting on her dishes,
the chef, Elka Gilmore, says: "Thanks to my dishes, make guests like to taste
foods even everyday." She combines finely barbecue or charcoal-baked smoked
cooking, which is widely accepted by Texan people, with her own sauce.
Her cooking won the 2nd prize at the 1987 American Seafood Challenge, and
the Grand Prix at the 1988 Californian Seafood Challenge, securing her an entry
right to the American Seafood Challenge.
Recently, many American women would like to become chefs, and she has been
recognized in America, as one of such successful female chefs. Landscape
photos displayed on the yellow wall are Jane Krensky's works colored by hand.
Together with the dishes of the chef Gilmore, these photos are creating an
artistic atmosphere.

Opened / December 1, 1987
Open /　11:30 a.m. to 2:30 p.m. (lunch: Monday to Friday)
　　　　6:00 p.m. to 10:30 p.m. (dinner: Sunday to Thursday)
　　　　6:00 p.m. to 11:30 p.m. (dinner: Friday · Saturday)
No. of guest seats / 40
Price per guest / entrée: $8 to 19,　dish: $50 to 70 (two guests)

左／乳牛たちの写真にさらに人工的に着色した Jane Krensky 氏の作品を飾る店内

Left / The inside display of Jane Krensky's pieces of art — artificially colored
　　photos of milch cow.

①

②

③

1／クラブケイク（カニ入りコロッケ）とオイスターシューターズ（スイートペッパーの酢とフィマ＝Jicamaソース）
2／トリブ（Halibut）魚のグリル　赤いピックルドオニオン　ズッキーニ添え　ビートのソース
3／チキンの胸肉のグリル（トマティーロソース）　コーンと赤いハレピーノ付き

The main dishes.

左／オープンキッチンの上に天窓を配した店内はカラフルで芸術的な雰囲気を演出している

Left / With a skylight above the open kitchen, the inside presents a colorful, artistic atmosphere.

若手女性オーナーシェフの Elka Gilmore さんとカラフルな店内　　　　The young female owner-chef, Ms. Elka Gilmore, and the colorful interior.

Left, bottom · right, bottom / Heavily employing barbecue or smoked cooking methods, the kitchen has a large grill. This restaurant serves wine and beer as drinks.

左下・右下／バーベキューやスモークの調理法を多くとり入れているキッチンでは大きなグリルが設置されている　当レストランの飲物はビールかワイン

炭焼きグリルの上部に天窓を設け　ダクトを配しているオープンキッチン　The open kitchen features a skylight and duct above the charcoal grill.

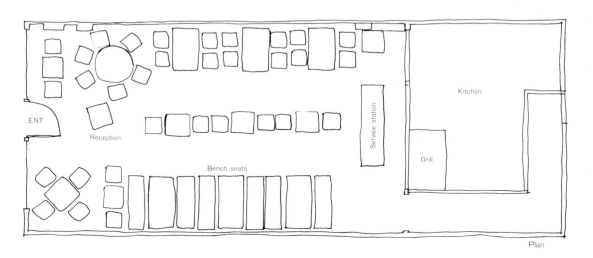

ENT

Reception

Bench seats

Service station

Kitchen

Grill

Plan

アーティスティックな外観の建物にはブティックや芸術家たちのオフィスがあり　その地階に当店はある
The building, having an artistic appearance, accommodates boutiques and artists' offices. This restaurant is at the basement.

水槽　音楽　写真作品が売りものの店内
The fish box, music and photographic pieces are attractions of this restaurant.

16 West Ontario Chicago, Illinois 60610　Phone/312-951-7979

写真作品の並ぶ壁面近くのテーブル席をみる　テーブルはイタリア製
The table seats near the wall on which photographic pieces are displayed.　The table is of Italian make.

700曲のＣＤミュージックボックスから流れる音楽が店内いっぱいに響きわたる　入口を入ったすぐ右のバーコーナー
Music from the CD music box (packing 700 pieces) is echoing throughout the inside.　Just to the right of the entrance is the bar corner.

アウト テイクス

"ギャラリー バー レストラン"というサブタイトルをつけたシカゴの新しい話題の店である。主に写真作品による展示会場内にバーとレストランを持ち込んだ店内構成となっている。店名の「アウト テイクス」とは撮影済みの写真の中から一番良いものだけを選び　他は捨て去るという意味で　ここでは現代写真家の作品を中心に展示し　販売もしている。
店内はバーコーナーとテーブル席で構成され　バーカウンターは水槽になっており　熱帯魚が泳いでいる。テーブルや椅子のデザインにも現代アートの感覚を取り入れたり700曲も導入されているコンパクトディスクからは店内に響きわたるほどのサウンドが聞こえる。バーコーナーを合わせて120席の店内は　ミドル エイジのプロフェッショナルやクリエイティブな仕事に携わる人達など600～900人の客で連日ごったがえしている。
料理は現在のところキッチンに強力な火が使用出来ないこともあってコールド ディッシュが中心であり　2.75～6.50ドルという幅のアイテムしか提供していない。それでも客単価は15～20ドルという手ごろなレストランである。
開店／1987年２月16日
営業時間／11:00AM～2:00AM
客席数／40席(テーブル席)　80席(バー)
客単価／15～20ドル(飲物含む)

OUT TAKES

A new topical shop in Chicago, subtitled "Gallery Bar Restaurant." The inside consists of a bar and a restaurant combined with the display space for photographs in the main. The shop name "Out Takes" means the choice of the best among photos that have been taken already, discarding the remaining ones. Here, the works of modern photographers are displayed and also sold in the main.
The inside consists of a bar corner and table seats. The bar counter includes a fish box featuring tropical fishes. The tables and chairs are designed with a modern and artistic sense, while sound from a compact disc packing 700 pieces of music is echoing throughout the shop. The inside has 120 seats including the bar corner, and is crowded everyday with 600 to 900 guests, including middle-aged professionals and those engaged in creative work.
At present, since the kitchen cannot use a strong fire, cold dishes are mainly served at the price range of from $2.75 to 6.50. The unit price per guest is moderate at $15 to 20.

Opened / February 16, 1987
Open / 11:00 a.m. to 2:00 a.m.
No. of guest seats / 40 (table seat), 80 (bar)
Price per guest / $15 to 20 (incl. drinks)

カウンターの水槽は毎時900ガロンの水が回転するように設計され　300匹の熱帯魚が遊泳しているのが楽しめる

The fish box at the counter is designed to cause 900 gallons of water circulate every hour, allowing guests to amuse watching 300 tropical fishes swimming.

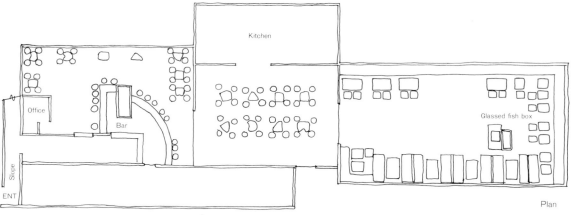

Plan

左・上／現代写真作家の作品展示と販売も兼ねるギャラリー風のバーコーナー

①

②

主な料理

1/ Three types of open sandwich.
2/ Tortellini juiienne veg dijon dressing.

Left・top / The gallery-style bar corner where pieces of contemporary photographers are exhibited and sold.

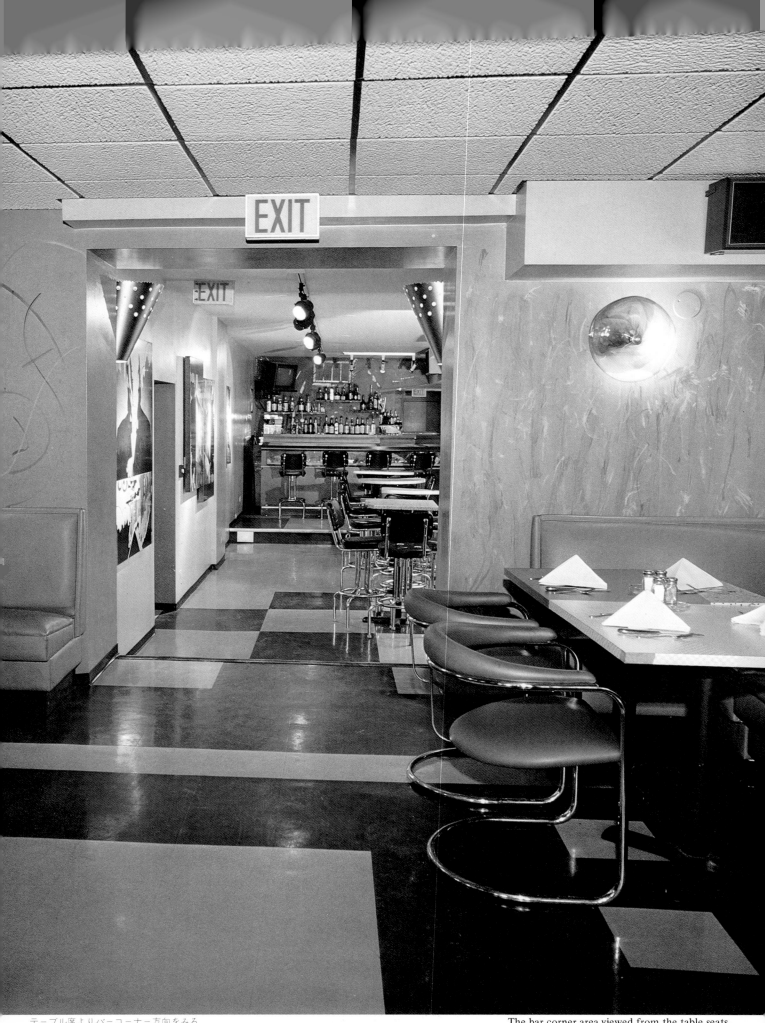

EXIT

テーブル席よりバーコーナー方向をみる

The bar corner area viewed from the table seats.

奥のテーブル席は深海を表現したコーナー

The inner table seat area is designed to express a deep-sea image.

左／地階の入口あたりの演出は水泡を表現している

Left / The entrance at the basement gives an image of bubbles.

ダイニングエリアにはビール名のネオンや懐かしい映画のポスターが飾られカジュアルな雰囲気を演出している
The dining area is decorated with neons bearing beer names and movie posters in good old days, presenting a casual atmopshere.

2347 Sepulveda West Los Angeles, CA 90025
Phone/206-644-9467

赤のテントと大きな店名のロゴを配したファサード
The facade with a red tent and a large logo of shop name.

天井の梁をそのまま見せてカジュアルな雰囲気を演出しているダイニングエリア
With the exposed ceiling beams, the dining area presents a casual atmosphere.

オーダーカウンターあたりより広い店内をみる

The wide inside scene viewed from the order counter.

ファサード

The facade.

手前に再注文のためのカウンターを設けて　サービスにつとめている

The order counter for re-order service stands in your side.

フレイキィ　ジェイクス

ダラスに本部を置き　約30店舗を展開するハンバーガーとベーカリーを中心としたファーストフード店で　ヤングアダルトやファミリー客をターゲットにしている。

グルメバーガーブームの最中であった1983年に設立され　インストアーベーカリーとブッチャーコーナーを設けている。サラダバーやハードリッカーを売るバーコーナーもあり　競合店より安い価格のメニューをセルフサービス方式の広い店内で提供している。ランチタイムには"5分間のランチを保証"というキャンペーンで　忙しいビジネス客の間で好評である。店内はビール名のネオンサインや懐かしい映画のポスターなどがいたるところに飾られ　カジュアルな雰囲気で"時間と安価"を売る店が強調されている。

営業時間／11：00AM～11：00PM(月～木)

11：00AM～12：00AM(金・土)

11：00AM～10：00PM(日)

客席数／242席(内ノースモーキングエリア54席)　26席(バーコーナー)

FLAKEY JAKE'S

Headquartered in Dallas, this fast food shop is developing a chain of about 30 shops, including hamburger and bakery shops in the main, intended for young adults and family guests.

Established in 1983 when the gourmet burger boom was at its height, it comprises an in-store bakery and butcher corner. A salad bar is also open, as well as a bar corner selling hard liquor. Menu items cheaper than competitors are served in the wide shop employing a self-service system. At the lunch time, a "5-minute lunch guarantee" campaign is favorably accepted by busy guests. The interior is decorated here and there with neon signs bearing beer names, movie posters of good old days, etc., thus stressing the shop feature that "time and cheap price" are sold in a casual atmosphere.

Open / 11:00 a.m. to 11:00 p.m. (Monday to Thursday)

11:00 a.m. to 12:00 a.m. (Friday · Saturday)

11:00 a.m. to 10:00 p.m. (Sunday)

No. of guest seats / 242 (incl. 54 seats in the no-smoking area)

26 (bar corner)

店内中央部に設けたスロープは車椅子の利用者を考えると同時に各コーナーを結ぶサービス通路にもなっている
The slope provided in the center of the restaurant is intended not merely for wheelchair users, but also serves as a service aisle connecting the different corners.

入口ドアを入ったあたりをみる　通路にはバーベキュー用の炭を置き　販売もしている

"5分間のランチ保証" は広いスペースのオーダーカウンターがあればこそ可能

Top / An area near the entrance door. Barbecue charcoal bags are placed along the aisle and sold.
Bottom / "5-minute lunch guarantee" is possible thanks to the spacious order counter.

"メディシンショップ" つまり薬屋というジョークを掲げたバーコーナー　　　The bar corner putting up "Medicine shop" i.e. drug store as a joke.

中央部通路に面し　2人用のテーブル席をうまく設けている

Facing the aisle in the center, table seats for two guests are neatly arranged.

サラダバー

The salad bar.

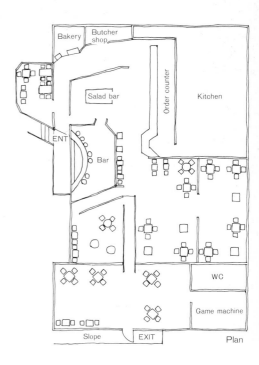

Plan

V字型に建つレストランのファサード

The V-shaped restaurant's facade.

バーコーナーは立飲み客があふれるほど賑わうため広いスペースを設けている

The bar corner is spaciously provided, since it is crowded so much that many guests drink standing.

 Jim McMahon's ..."one of a kind!"

1970 North Lincoln Ave. Chicago, Illinois 60614
Phone/312-751-1700

フットボールやメガホンを飾ったバーのサービスエリア

The service area of the bar decorated with footballs, megaphones, etc.

4PM TO 6PM

THEISMANN 7

パブ感覚のバーコーナーの一角

Part of the bar corner having an atmosphere of pub.

ジム マクマホンズ

シカゴを中心に話題のレストラン コンセプトを
つくり出している「Lettuce Entertain You社」
は「Ed Debevic's」「Cafe Ba-Bareeba」「Scoozi」
などに続いて1987年の春 "スポーツ界の輝かし
い思い出"をテーマとしたインテリアのこの「ジム
マクマホンズ」をオープンした。
1階をバーとダイニングとし 地下は "プレス
クラブ" と名付けた90席のプライベート パー
ティ専用のダイニングエリアを備えている。オ
ーナーのジム マクマホンは"シカゴベアーズ"
で活躍した有名なフットボールプレイヤーであ
るが 店内は4半世紀にわたる数々の写真やユ
ニフォームのコレクションがいっぱいに飾られ
ている。彼のファンやスポーツ愛好者たちがよ
くこの店を訪れる。
料理はオール アメリカンメニューで アントレ
が5～16ドルといったポピュラープライスの気
軽に利用できるレストランである。
開店／1987年4月13日
営業時間／11:30AM～ 2:00PM(ランチ　月～金)
　　　　　 5:30PM～11:00PM(ディナー 月～木)
　　　　　11:30AM～ 1:00AM(土)
　　　　　11:30AM～11:00PM(日)
客席数／1階242席　地下90席(バンケットルー
ム)

入口近くには店名の入ったTシャツやキャラクターグッズを売るコーナーがある
Near the entrance is a corner selling T-shirts bearing the shop name, and character goods.

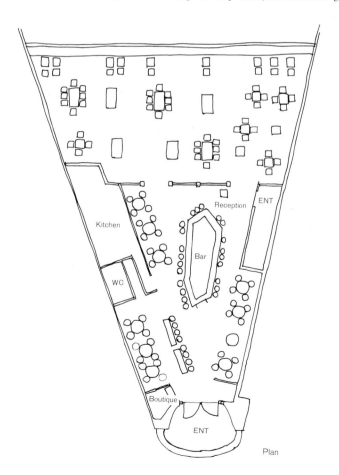

Plan

JIM MCMAHON'S

Creating a topical restaurant concept mainly
in Chicago, "Lettuce Entertain You" compa-
ny opened this "Jim McMahon's," featuring
the interior whose theme is "brilliant memo-
ries of the sports world," in the spring of
1987, following "Ed Debevic's," "Cafe Ba-
Bareeba," "Scoozi," etc.
With the bar and dining occupying the 1st
floor, the basement is used by "Press Club,"
a dining area with 90 seats specially used for
private party. Jim McMahon, is a famous
football player who was once active with the
"Chicago Bears." The interior is decorated
with many photos, uniform collection, etc.
extending over a quarter century. This shop
is frequented by his fans and sports fans.
The menu consists of all American dishes
served at popular prices, including $5 to 16
for entrée. This is a casual restaurant that can
be used in a relaxing manner.

Opened / April 13, 1987
Open /　11:30 a.m. to 2:00 p.m.
　　　　　(lunch: Monday to Friday)
　　　　　5:30 p.m. to 11:00 p.m.
　　　　　(dinner: Monday to Thursday)
　　　　　11:30 a.m. to 1:00 a.m. (Saturday)
　　　　　11:30 a.m. to 11:00 p.m.
　　　　　(Sunday)
No. of guest seats /　1st floor: 242
　　　　　　　　　　 Basement: 90
　　　　　　　　　　　(banquet room)

110席の1階奥にあるダイニングエリアは木製フロア

The wooden floor of the dining area with 110 seats at an inner part of the 1st floor.

パブ感覚のバーコーナーの一角　　　　　　　　Part of the bar corner.

①

②

③

赤と白を用いた清潔感のある明るいトイレ　　The clean toilet with red & white coloring.

1／野菜類のグリルプレイト
2／マンゴとベビーレタス　トマト　カットステーキのスペシャルサラダ
3／チキンの胸肉をマッシュルームのソテー・レモンバターソースかけ

The main dishes.

メルローズ通りに面した白いモダンな造りのファサード　　The white, modern facade facing Mellose Street.

ロスのモダンアーティストによる作品が入口に立ち印象づける
The impressive pieces of modern artists in Los Angeles standing by the entrance.

CITRUS

6703 Melrose Ave. Los Angeles, CA 90038
Phone/213-857-0034

74

エントランスホール後方のテラス風ダイニング

The terrace-like dining behind the entrance hall.

オープンキッチンが見えるテラス風ダイニングルーム　　　　The terrace-like dining room where the open kitchen is visible.

The formal dining area spreading in your side over the entrance hall and bar area. Behind them is the terrace-like dining.

上／エントランスホール　バーエリアをはさんで手前に広がるフォーマルな感じのダイニング　後方にテラス風ダイニング

左／モダンアートの絵が飾ってあるダイニングルーム　右にレセプション

The dining room decorated with modern artistic pictures. The reception at right.

レセプションあたりよりみるバーと右側にダイニングエリア

The bar and dining at right viewed from the reception area.

シトラス

いまロサンゼルスでもっともホットなレストランとして話題になっているのがこの店だ。店名は"柑きつ類"という意味。

オーナー シェフであるミシェル リチャード（Michel Richard）氏はフランスの大西洋に面したブルターニュ地方の生まれで 料理人としての経験をフランスを中心に過ごし 1974年にニューヨークへやって来た。以後サンタ フェ ニュー メキシコ ロサンゼルスと移り ケーキとデザートの専門店を開店したり 料理コンサルタントとしての仕事も多く手がけてきた料理人である。

39歳の時 彼は"カリフォルニアを十分に理解し リラックスした楽しい時を過ごせる雰囲気の中で 美味い料理を提供しよう"というコンセプトで「シトラス」を開店した。

店内はホワイトを基調にし カリフォルニアらしい明るい空間に モダンでアーティスティックなインテリアで構成している。大きなテントが並ぶ左のダイニングルームからはオープンキッチンが見えるし 中央の

バーコーナーから右側の部屋はモダンな造りの中に現代アーティストによる絵が飾ってある。

シェフの調理法はバターやクリームは使用せず ソースはコンソメをベースに野菜類のピューレやオリーブオイルを多用するのが特徴。健康やカロリー指向に味と色彩を加えた料理が好評である。

開店／1987年2月1日

営業時間／12：00PM～ 3：00PM（ランチ）
　　　　　 6：30PM～11：00PM（ディナー）
　　　　　 2：00AMまで（バー）

休日／日曜 祭日

客席数／190席

従業員数／85人

客単価／ランチ20ドル ディナー35ドル（飲物含む）

レストラン中央部に設けられたデザートカウンターとバー   The dessert counter and bar provided in the center of the restaurant.

CITRUS

This restaurant is drawing now much attention in Los Angeles. The shop's name suggests its concept.

Michel Richard, owner-chef, was born in Bretagne, France, facing The Atlantic Ocean. After improving his skill as a cook mainly in France, he came over to New York in 1974. Since then, he has moved to Santa Fe, New Mexico and Los Angeles, either opening confectionery & dessert shops or developing his career as a cooking consultant. At the age of 39, he opened "Citrus" with the following concept: "Serve delicious dishes in a relaxed, amusing atmosphere, by fully appreciating California." Using white as the basic tone, the interior features a modern, artistic arrangement in a bright space peculiar to California. The open kitchen can be observed from the left-hand dining room with large tents. The room in the right side of the central bar corner features a modern style while displaying paintings of contemporary artists.

The chef does not use butter or cream, but a great amount of purée of vegetable based on consommé, and olive oil. Health and calorie oriented dishes with taste and color are well accepted.

Opened / February 1, 1987
Open /   12:00 p.m. to 3:00 p.m. (lunch)
          6:30 p.m. to 11:00 p.m. (dinner)
          Up to 2:00 a.m. (bar)
Closed / Sunday, holiday
No. of guest seats / 190
No. of employees / 85
Price per guests / lunch: $20,   dinner: $35 (incl. drink)

ワインセラーを含むフルバーと入口方向をみる

The full bar, including a wine cellar, and entrance area.

主な料理

1/ Crab cole slan.
2/ Sauteed mahi-mahi with ginger scallion sauce.
3/ Lamb loin with tomato.
4/ Smoked salmon terrine

オーナーシェフの Michel Richard 氏を中央にしたクルーたち

The crew with Michel Richard, owner-chef, in the center.

ワインセラーをもつバーサービスエリア

The bar service area with a wine cellar.

デザートのディスプレイカウンター
The dessert display counter.

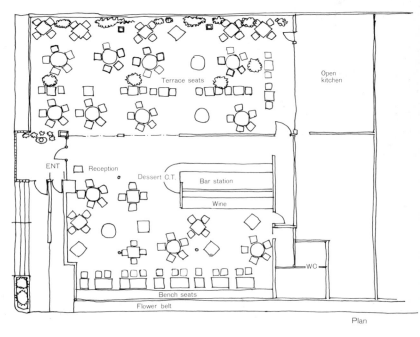

Plan

エントランスホールにある　おだやかな表情の木彫りの仏像たちが客を迎えてくれる
The mild-faced wooden Buddhist images welcome guests at the entrance.

ウイルシャー通り（Wilshire Blvd.）に面したオフィスビルの1階に出店
Opened at the 1st floor of an office building facing Wilshire Blvd.

FRAGRANT VEGETABLE
RESTAURANT/香齋厨

11859 Wilshire Blvd. Los Angeles, CA 90025　Phone/213-312-1442

料理は精進料理に由来し　野菜のみで調理する広東スタイルのレストラン（120席）
Dished served at this Kwangtung style restaurant are modeled after so-called "shojin" (vegetable) dishes using vegetables alone (120 seats).

香齋厨

使用食材は野菜だけというニューコンセプトのチャイニーズレストラン
がロサンゼルスに出現して話題になっている。

中華料理には　海老　あわび　牛肉　豚肉　家鴨といったあらゆる魚介
や肉が使われるが「香齋厨」では不思議なことにそれらの素材は一切使
用されず　材料はすべて野菜である。たとえば豚肉のかわりにグルテン
を使ったり　牛肉のかわりに豆腐　あわびや海老はマッシュルームで作
る。化学調味料もまったく使わず　油もコーンオイルだけを用いるなど
徹底したヘルシーコンセプトである。

これらは　インド仏教伝来のいわゆる精進料理に由来し　この店独自の
調理方法を研究した結果から生み出されたという。

このような店は香港などではいくつ見られるが　アメリカには　ニュー
ヨークやワシントンD.C.に数ヵ所ある程度で　南カリフォルニアには初
めて出現した。中華料理の新しいコンセプトとして多くのマスコミにも
とり上げられている話題のレストランだ。

開店／1987年11月1日
営業時間／11:30AM～ 2:30PM（ランチ）
　　　　　 5:30PM～10:30PM（ディナー：月～木・土）
　　　　　 5:30PM～11:00PM（ディナー：金・土）
客席数／120席
従業員数／11人

FRAGRANT VEGETABLE RESTAURANT

A new-concept Chinese restaurant using only vegetables as materials,
this restaurant opened in Los Angeles is becoming very popular.
Usually, Chinese dishes use all types of fish and meat, such as shrimps,
abalone, beef, pork and chicken. Strangely enough, at this "Fragrant
Vegetable Restaurant," none of these materials are used, but only
vegetables are used. For instance, gluten is used instead of pork,
bean curd 'tofu' instead of beef, and abalone and shrimps are made
from mushroom. Only corn oil is used instead of artificial seasonings.
This is indeed a thorough-going health-oriented concept!
These originate from so-called 'shojin' (vegetable) dishes handed down
from the Indian Buddhism, and are the products of this restaurant's
own cooking method.
Although several restaurants of this type are open in Hong Kong, etc.,
there are only a few in the U.S. (New York, Washington D.C., etc.).
This restaurant appeared in South California for the first time. As
a restaurant with a new concept of Chinese dishes, it is reported by
TV and other mass media, drawing wide attention.

Opened / November 1, 1987
Open /　11:30 a.m. to 2:30 p.m. (lunch)
　　　　5:30 p.m. to 10:30 p.m.
　　　　　(dinner: Monday to Thursday · Saturday)
　　　　5:30 p.m. to 11:00 p.m. (dinner: Friday · Saturday)
No. of guest seats / 120
No. of employees / 11

ブース席より店内奥をみる

The inner part viewed from the booth seat area.

カットグラスを使用したエレガントで明るい窓際のテーブル席（全客席ノースモーキング）
The elegant and bright window-side table seats using cut glass (no smoking at all seats).

レセプションに近い客席コーナーは　より明るい雰囲気で仏教の世界を表現した絵が壁面いっぱいに飾られている
The guest seat corner close to the reception features many paintings on the wall expressing the Buddhist world in a brighter atmosphere.

① ② ③

１・２・３／材料は野菜のみ　化学調味料　肉　魚介類は一切使用せず　徹底したヘルシーコンセプトが特徴

1, 2, 3 / Only vegetables are used as materials. Neither chemical seasonings nor meet, fish and shellfish are used. The perfect health concept characterizes this restaurant's dishes.

嘉陵鳥
西方秉畫
面相偎
澄波美笑
芸芸新荳院
豆角

テーブル席より壁面にそったブース席をみる

The booth seats along the wall viewed from the table seats.

上下できるシェイドがヘルシーな明るさを強調している窓際のテーブル席
The window-side table seats feature a shade that can be raised/lowered.

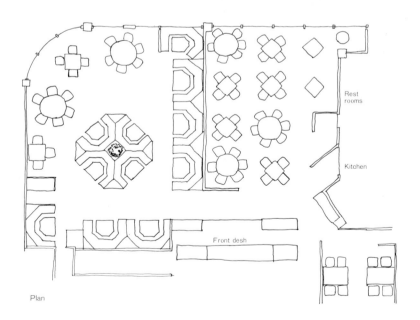

Rest rooms

Kitchen

Front desh

Plan

夕方になるとテラスを利用したカクテルコーナーが設けられる　後方のビルの中央部がレストランの入口
In the evening a cocktail corner utilizing the terrace space is opened. In the center of the building at the back is the entrance to the restaurant.

バーカウンターより入口方向をみる　奥のダイニングエリアまで広く通路をとっている
The entrance area viewed from the bar counter. A wide aisle is secured leading to the inner dining area.

CHINA GRILL

60 West 53rd St. (between 5 th & 6 th Ave.) New York, N.Y. 10019
Phone/212-333-7788

レセプションのすぐ右側の一段高くなったダイニングエリア　左奥にバー　オープンキッチンと続く
The dining area a little above the surrounding floor just in the right side of the reception, followed by the bar and open kitchen in the inner left areas.

オープンキッチンをはさんで右と左にバーカウンターが設けられている　The bar counters in the right and left sides sandwiching the open kitchen.

チャイナグリル

この「チャイナ グリル」の魅力は　日本　中国　インドネシア　ベトナム　フランスなどの料理と　カリフォルニア料理をブレンドして　まったく新しいスタイルの料理 "インターナショナル フード" を生み出したところにある。

日本人のシェフ　田中誠人 (Mako Tanaka) 氏は渡米9年「チャイナ グリル」を開店する前の3年半はサンタモニカの「Chinois on Main」(「Spago's」の経営者 Wolfgang Puck 氏の店でもある) で働いていた。当然その間の経験がこの店のダイナミックな料理にも反映している。

モダーンアート美術館の近くにあるこのレストランの店内のデコアは高い天井空間の上部に日本の障子を思わせる楕円形の大きなランプシェードが印象的だ。おさえぎみの壁面カラーと幾つかに分けられた客席　中央部に設けたオープンキッチンとその両側にある細長いバーカウンターなどで構成されている。

開店／1987年9月25日
営業時間／12:00PM～ 2:30PM (ランチ　月～金)
　　　　　5:00PM～11:00PM (ディナー　月～水)
　　　　　6:00PM～12:30AM (ディナー　日)
客席数／185席　40席 (バー)
従業員数／125人 (キッチン65人　サービス60人)
客単価／ランチ25～35ドル　ディナー40～50ドル

CHINA GRILL

This "China Grill" is attractive since it offers completely new-styled "international foods" by blending Japanese, Chinese, Indonesian, Vietnamese, French and other dishes, with Californian dishes.

Before opening "China Grill" nine years after his arrival in the U.S., Japanese chef, Mako Tanaka, had served "Chinois on Main" (the shop of Wolfgang Puck, owner of "Spago's") in Santa Monica, for three years and a half. His experience in those years naturally is reflected in delicious dishes served by this restaurant.

The decor in this restaurant near the Modern Art Museum is impressive with a large oval lampshade at an upper part of the high ceiling space that reminds us of Japanese 'shoji' (paper sliding screen). The moderate wall colors and guest seats in several partitions, the open kitchen in the center, the narrow bar counters in both sides of the open kitchen, etc. compose the inside space.

Opened / September 25, 1987
Open /　12:00 p.m. to 2:30 p.m. (lunch: Monday to Friday)
　　　　5:00 p.m. to 11:00 p.m. (dinner: Monday to Wednesday)
　　　　6:00 p.m. to 12:30 a.m. (dinner: Sunday)
No. of guest seats / 185, 40 (bar)
No. of employees / 125 (kitchen: 65, service men: 60)
Price per guest / lunch: $25 to 35, dinner: $40 to 50

店内中央部に設けたバーカウンターとオープンキッチン　フロアの黒く見える線にはマルコポーロの「東方見聞録」が英語で書かれ奥へとつながる
The bar counter and open kitchen provided in the center. Along the dark lines on the floor are written Marco Polo's "Record of Experiences in the East" in English, leading to the inner part.

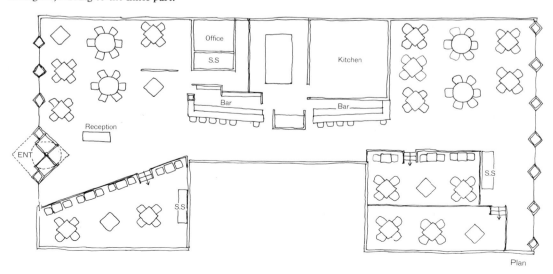

Plan

①

②

③

主な料理

1/ Grill quail in nest.
2/ Peking duck salad.
3/ Grill marinated lamb.

左／店内奥のダイニングエリア　フロアに段差をつけて　天井の高さをうまく
利用している

Left / The inner dining area. Using a difference in floor level, the
　　ceiling height is effectively utilized.

障子をイメージしたというランプシェードや大きな花の飾りがあるレセプション近くのダイニングエリア
The dining area near the reception featuring a shade designed by using an image of "shoji" (paper sliding screen), large floor decoration, etc.

天井の高い店内をすっきり見せる壁面の装飾
The wall decoration helps giving a clear view of the inside whose ceiling is high.

店内奥のダイニングエリアよりバー　キッチン　入口方向をみる
The bar, kitchen and entrance areas viewed from the inner dining area.

ファサード　グリーンを這わせた外装の中にアイアンとブラスで構成したロゴ
The facade. The exterior with green, and the logotype composed of iron and brass.

The 1st floor bar area having an elegant atmosphere.

コーナーに建つレストランの外観はまるで住宅のようだ
Standing at a corner, the restaurant looks like a mansion.

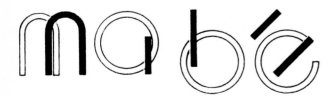

8722 West 3rd Street Los Angeles, CA 90048
Phone/213-276-6223

The bar lounge's wall surface is mirror-finished to give a spacious impression.

エレガントな雰囲気の1階バーエリア

美しいファブリックのブース席と階段横のサービスステーション
The booth seats using beautiful fabric, and service station beside the staircase.

バーラウンジの壁面は鏡をかけて店内の広がりを演出

1階奥のダイニングエリアよりブース席をみる
The booth seats viewed from the dining area at an inner part of the 1st floor.

模様を織り込んだじゅうたんを敷き詰めた明るいエレガントな1階ダイニングエリア
The bright, elegant dining area at the 1st floor covered up with pattern-woven carpet.

大きな窓を設けた開放的なダイニングエリア

The open dining area with a large window.

マベ

「マベ」とは未完成の真珠という意味だが　店内のデコアや料理　サービス共に完成度の高いレストランとして好評である。コンテンポラリィ/クラシックといったいかにも女性客が好みそうな店内の雰囲気は　まるでリッチな人たちの家の中を想い出させるようでもある。一方オープンでカジュアルなカリフォルニアの雰囲気もとり入れることを忘れていない。料理はというとフランス料理とイタリア料理をうまく結び合わせて構成しているところも　トレンディな感覚を与える。さらに客にとってうれしいことは　料理のすばらしさに対して　比較的安さを感じるということ。これは最近の傾向として外食をする人たちが増えてきており　一回に費やす予算がさがってきているという背景も店側が考慮しているからだ。
ビバリーヒルズやウエストハリウッド周辺からの　リッチでナイスピープルといわれる客が好んで利用しているが　このクラスのレストランとしては　非常にリーズナブルな客単価で　ランチ約18ドルディナー約30ドルである。

開店／1988年8月23日
営業時間／11:00AM～3:00PM（ランチ：月～土）
　　　　　5:30PM～2:00AM（ディナー）
　　　　　11:00AM～3:00PM（ブランチ：日）
客席数／160席
従業員数／65人
客単価／ランチ 18ドル　ディナー 30ドル

MABÉ

Though "Mabé" as its name means imperfect pearl, this restaurant is accepted favorably as one that has achieved a high degree of perfection in the décor, dish and service. With an atmosphere that may be expressed as something like "contemporary-classic," the inside appears to be very attractive to female guests, since it makes us feel as if we are in a high class residence. Meanwhile, the owner has also introduced an open and casual Californian atmosphere. A tasty combination of French and Italian dishes gives also a "trendy" feeling. What's more pleasing to guests is that dishes, though wonderful, seem to be priced moderately. This is due to the considerations given by the restaurant to the fact that diners-out are increasing recently and their budget per a meal is decreasing.
This restaurant is frequented by so-called "rich and nice people" from Beverly Hills, West Hollywood, etc. For this class of restaurant, the unit prices per guest are very reasonable – about $18 for lunch and $30 for dinner.

Opened / August 23, 1988
Open / 11:00 a.m. to 3:00 a.m. (lunch: Monday to Saturday)
　　　　5:30 p.m. to 2:00 a.m. (dinner)
　　　　11:00 a.m. to 3:00 p.m. (brunch: Sunday)
No. of guest seats / 160
No. of employees / 65
Price per guest / lunch: $18,　dinner: $30

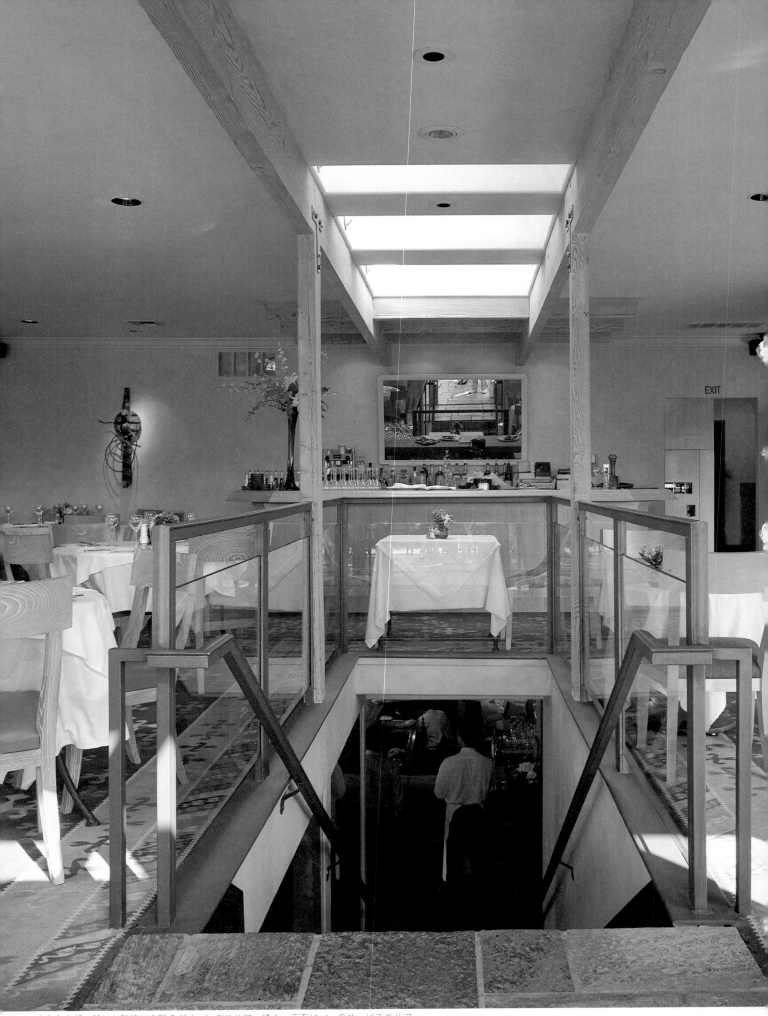

店内中央部に設けた階段は2階のダイニングエリアへ続く　正面はバーのサービスエリア
The staircase provided in the center leads to the 2nd floor's dining area.　Visible in front of you is a service area of the bar.

トレンディなフランス料理で人気のある当店のシェフ Claude Segal 氏とポピュラーメニュー
The chef, Claude Segal, who is popular for trendy French dishes, and his popular menu.

暖炉を配しエレガントな雰囲気の2階ラウンジ
The 2nd floor lounge has an elegant atmosphere with a fireplace.

1階と同様に開放的でアットホームな感じの2階ダイニングエリア
The 2nd floor dining area has an open, homely atmosphere, just like the 1st floor.

壁面にはモダンアートの作品が飾られ　夜ともなれば一段と浮き上って目立つライティングとなる
The walls are decorated with pieces of modern art, and at right they change into very showy lighting.

オープンエアのテラス席　上部にはヒーターが設置されている
The terrace seats on the open area, with a heater installed above.

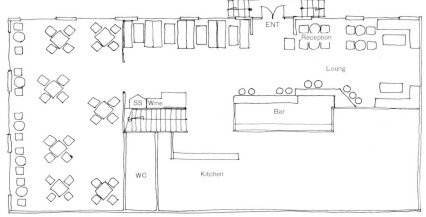

1F Plan

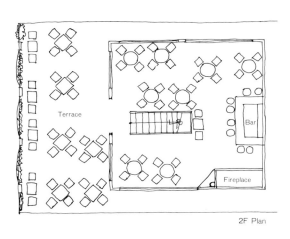

2F Plan

サンタモニカの海辺に高級レストランが出店してきている その中の一角にカフェ レストランの雰囲気をもたせ オーシャン アベニューに面したファサード

白い壁面と白いテーブルクロスが店内を一層明るく感じさす テラスダイニングエリアよりみるレセプション

OPERA

1551 Ocean Ave. Santa Monica, CA
Phone/231-393-9224

Top / Into the beach of Santa Monica are appearing high-class restaurants. Among them stands the facade of this restaurant facing the Ocean Avenue, and it looks like a cafe restaurant.

Bottom / The white wall and white table cloth make the inside even more bright. The reception viewed from the terrace dining area.

明るい開放的な店内はカジュアルな雰囲気で南欧風の料理が味わえる
In the bright, open space with a casual atmosphere, you can taste South European dishes.

カジュアルな地中海風レストランの店内にはサンタモニカの風が流れる
Through the casual, mediterranean restaurant, the wind of Santa Monica is blowing.

オペラ

サンタモニカの太平洋に面した埠頭近くに格調のあるレストランが集まる一角が出現した。その中に出店した一つのレストランが当地ロサンゼルスで有名な「トランプス(Trumps)」のオーナーたちが経営する 新しい料理のコンセプトを売りだした「オペラ」である。

南フランスのコート ダジュールやリビエラを想い出させるような立地条件を備えたサイド ウォーク カフェのようなレストランであり 開放的な店内の雰囲気は周囲の環境によく溶け込ませている。料理はもちろん地中海風のものを中心に スペインやイタリア 北アフリカ ギリシャといった地域の料理などを独自のスタイルにして幅広く提供している。

シェフのDon Dickmanは本店「トランプス」のシェフMichael Robertsの下で働いていた 期待されている料理人である。

開店／1988年8月

営業時間／11：30AM～ 2：30PM（ランチ：月～土）
　　　　　6：00PM～10：30PM（ディナー：日～木）
　　　　　6：00PM～11：00PM（ディナー：金・土）
　　　　　10：30AM～ 2：30PM（ブランチ：日）

客席数／110席
客単価／ランチ 25～50ドル（2人）　ディナー 40～65ドル（2人）

レストラン全体を見渡せるバーカウンターが店内中央に位置する

The bar counter overlooking the restaurant as a whole is set in the center.

OPERA

In Santa Monica, near a pier facing the Pacific Ocean, a corner has appeared where dignified restaurants are in operation. "Opera" is one of these restaurants managed by the owners of "Trumps" that is well-known in Los Angeles, and features new-concept dishes. Just like a sidewalk cafe, this restaurant is located in an environment that reminds us of Côte d'Azur or Riviera in South France, and its inside atmosphere blends well with the surrounding scenery. In addition to Mediterranean dishes served in the main, Spanish, Italian, North African, Greek and other dishes are also available in unique styles. Don Dickman, the chef, is a very promising cook who has been working under Michael Roberts, chef of "Trumps" — main restaurant.

Opened / August 1988
Open /   11:30 a.m. to 2:30 p.m. (lunch: Monday to Saturday)
         6:00 p.m. to 10:30 p.m. (dinner: Sunday to Thursday)
         6:00 p.m. to 11:00 p.m. (dinner: Friday · Saturday)
         10:30 a.m. to 2:30 p.m. (brunch: Sunday)
No. of guest seats / 110
Price per guest / lunch: $25 to 50 (two guests),
                 dinner: $40 to 65 (two guests)

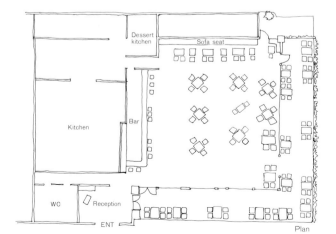

Plan

サンタモニカの海辺に面したレストランは窓も大きく開放的　　　　　　　　Facing the beach of Santa Monica, the restaurant has large open windows.

①

②

③

1／ライム Zabaglione のグラタン　ブルーベリー添え　タンジェリン　ナポレオンバ
　　ターソースのデザート
2／オリーブオイル　ガーリック　ハーブなどで調理した地中海産野菜のベイクに
　　盛り付けした帆立貝のロースト
3／ひな鳥とチキンのパイ皮包み揚げ

The main dishes.

ファサード　以前は自動車のショールームだったところをレストランに改装

エントランス廻り

Top / The facade. The automobile showroom has been redecorated into a restaurant.
Bottom / Around the entrance.

1415 Van Ness San Francisco, CA 94109　Phone/415-928-7188

ブリキ製の椰子の木に囲まれたモノトーンの店内中央部ダイニングエリア　　The central monotone dining area surrounded with tin-made coconut trees.

入口右側のコーナーがバー　ゆったりした籐椅子があり　その後方の窓側にブリキ製のカウンター
In the right side of the entrance is a bar corner, with comfortable cane chairs, behind which is a tin-made counter along the window.

サーカスのテントを思わせるエントランスホールよりダイニングエリアへの入口をみる

ロザリーズ

店舗の演出　それは客にとってもレストラン側にとっても大きな関心事である。以前日本の化粧品会社のモデルをしたことのあるオーナーのBill Belloli氏は　日本通として知られるが　自ら店づくりのアイディアを出し　まるで自分の子供を見守るように毎日店に顔を出す。

広い空間の店内はブリキの板のヤシの木やテーブルトップが目立つモノトーンカラーで構成し　裸のマネキンがパーティションの上部にぶら下がっているなどユニークな演出をしている。独特のユーモアと個性を持ち込んだこの「ロザリーズ」がいまサンフランシスコのトレンディレストランとして話題になっている。

料理にも新しいスタイルを持ち　いろいろな素材やフレイバーを一つの皿に盛り合わせ手の込んだメニューづくりをしており　毎月メニューを変えるなど熱心なところも人気のひとつとなっているようだ。

開店／1985年5月20日
営業時間／11：30AM～ 2：30PM（ランチ：月～土）
　　　　　　5：30PM～10：30PM（ディナー：月～日）
客席数／170席（レストラン）　10席（バー）

ブリキ製のバーカウンターやランプシェードのクールさを籐のスツールのホットさで補う　ボトルの上にマネキンのぶらさがりがみえる
The coolness of the tin-made bar counter and lampshade is compensated for by the hotness of cane stool. Visible above the bottles is a suspended mannequin.

従業員数／75人
客単価／ランチ18.50ドル　ディナー38.50ドル（飲物含む）

ROSALIE'S

The shop presentation is a major concern for both guests and restaurant. Mr. Bill Belloli, the owner, worked once as a model for a Japanese cosmetic manufacturer, is known for his wide knowledge about Japan. Presenting his own ideas on shop making, he drops in the restaurant everyday, and moves about as if watching his own child.

The spacious inside is composed of monotone colors on tin plates for coconut trees, tabletop finish, etc., and naked mannequins are suspended from the upper parts of the partitions. "Rosalie's" is drawing much attention as a "trendy" restaurant in San Francisco, thanks to its unique presentation, humor and individuality.

Introducing various new styles of dish, such as dishing up various types of material and flavor over a plate, the menu making is very sophisticated, and the contents are changed every month. This

enthusiasm seems to be another reason for the popularity of this restaurant.

Opened / May 20, 1985
Open /　11:30 a.m. to 2:30 p.m. (lunch: Monday to Saturday)
　　　　　5:30 p.m. to 10:30 p.m. (dinner: Monday to Sunday)
No. of guest seats / 170 (restaurant),　10 (bar)
No. of employees / 75
Price per guest / lunch: $18.50,　dinner $38.50 (incl. drink)

Left page, bottom / The entrance to the dining area viewed from that entrance hall that reminds us of a circus tent.

117

①

②

③

1／スチームしたアスパラガスのフィロ（Phyllo）包み　バルメザンチーズかけのベイク
2／ポークの腰肉のスモーク　ブラウンシュガーとバーボンソース
3／ビーフのヒレ　ポートワインとグレープソース　ワイルドライスの葉包みとイエロービース添え

The main dishes.

左／段差を設けた客席と広い空間の中にマネキンを配してユーモアのある遊び感覚を表現

Left / The guest seat area differing in level, with a sense of humorous play **by** arranging mannequins in the wide space.

段差のあるテーブル席は柱のない広さを感じる空間に展開され　ブリキ製の椰子の木やマネキンが目立つ　手前はPOSによるオーダーシステムを採用している　キッチンとキャッシャーにも直結している

白いピローケースが並ぶピアノラウンジ　ランチとディナータイムにライブのピアノ演奏がある
The piano lounge with a row of white pillow cases. A live piano performance is offered at lunch time and dinner time.

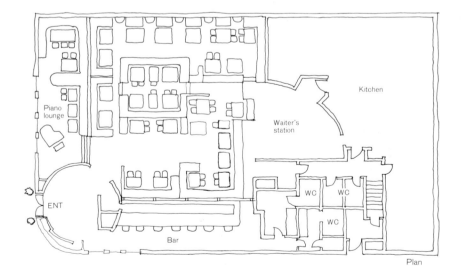

Left / Differing in level, the table seat area is developed over a wide space without pillars, and accented with tin-made coconut trees and mannequins. The area in your side directly leads to the kitchen and cashier operated by POS order system.

ファサード　マンハッタン　パーク　アベニューのビルの1・2階にある

The facade. Placed at the 1st and 2nd floors of a building at Manhattan Park Ave.

235 Park Ave.(South at 19th St.) New York, N.Y. 10003
Phone/212-529-4770

エントランス上部にはブラス製の10フィートもあるイグアナがトロピカルな雰囲気の中に置かれ　外からも目立つ

On the upper part of the entrance is visibly placed a huge (10-feet) brass-made iguana in a tropical atmosphere.

店内中央部階段よりエントランス廻りをみる   The entrance area viewed from the staircase in the center of the restaurant.

カフェ イグアナ

マンハッタンのミッドタウンの南にオープンした「カフェ イグアナ」は
オーナーの Joyce Steins さんが最も魅惑された映画"イグアナの夜"のシ
ーンを再現したレストラン　300席もある大きな店内に10フィートのブラ
ス製のイグアナが目をひく。
トロピカルな雰囲気のダイニングエリア　ステージ状に展開するフロア構
成　その中に色とりどりのユニークな照明を施し12個のスピーカーから
流れる音楽はオーナーの好きなクラシックからスティングまで400本のカ
セットから選ばれる。夜の10時きっかりにはＤＪの高らかな声が店内い
っぱいにスピンする。
メニューはバケーション料理とでも呼ばれるようなカジュアルで楽しさ
を盛り込んだ Tex Mex とグリル料理が多く Tax Mex 料理にはメキシカ
ンライス　ブラックビーンズとトルティーヤが２枚ついてくる。飲物で
はメキシカンビールやフローズン マルガリータが売物で　特にイグアナ
リータというハウス スペシャルのマルガリータに人気がある。
開店／1988年１月11日
営業時間／11:30AM〜 4:00PM（ランチ：月〜金）
　　　　　　4:00PM〜12:30AM（ディナー：土〜木）
　　　　　　4:00PM〜 1:30AM（ディナー：金〜土）
　　　　　12:00PM〜 4:00PM（ブランチ：土・日）
客席数／300席（ダイニングエリアのみ）他にバーコーナーあり

CAFE IGUANA

Opened in the south of Midtown, Manhattan, "Cafe Iguana" is a large
restaurant (300 seats) featuring an inside arrangement of scenes of
"The Night of Iguana," a picture that has inspired the owner Joyce
Steins. The 10-feet iguana made of brass is very conspicuous, among
others.
The dining area has a tropical atmosphere, and the floor composition
is developed like a stage provided with a variety of unique lighting.
And music delivered from twelve speakers is selected from among 400
members including classic and even "sting" loved by the owner. Just
on 10 p.m. DJ's high voice spins round.
The menu contains dishes that may be called a "vacation dish,"
centering around Tex-Mex and grill dishes that are casual and full of
pleasure. Tex-Mex dish is served together with Mexican rice, black
beans and two plates of tortilla. Drinks are composed of Mexican
beer, frozen margarita, etc. A special margarita called "Iguanarita" is
very popular, among others.

Opened / January 11, 1988
Open / 11:30 a.m. to 4:00 p.m. (lunch: Monday to Friday)
         4:00 p.m. to 12:30 a.m. (dinner: Saturday to Thursday)
         4:00 p.m. to 1:30 a.m. (dinner: Friday · Saturday)
         12:00 p.m. to 4:00 p.m. (brunch: Saturday · Sunday)
No. of guest seats / 300 (dining area only); a bar corner provided

2階のベランダ席（40席）をみる   The veranda area (40 seats) on the 2nd floor.

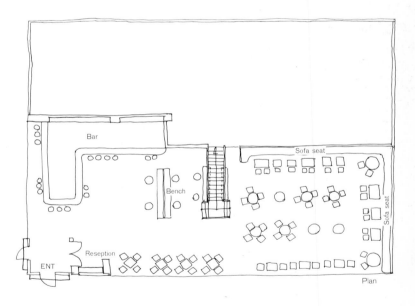

900平方フィート（約836.1㎡）の広々とした空間に映画"ナイト オブ イグアナ"のシーンを再現した　中央部の階段を登るとベランダ　トロピカルバーとレストラン　バルコニーレベルのカンクンルームなどに通じる

The scenes of the movie "Night of Iguana" are reproduced on the wide space, 900 square feet (about 836.1 m²). Climbing the central staircase, it leads to the veranda, tropical bar, restaurant, counter room at the balcony level, etc.

1階バーコーナー越しに中央階段方向をみる　大きなクリスタル製のイグアナが強い印象を残す
The central staircase area viewed across the 1st floor bar corner. The large crystal iguana is very impressive.

オーナーのコレクション400本のカセットから選ばれる音楽とＤＪがこのコーナーに集まる人たちを酔わせる
Music from the owner's collection of 400 cassettes and DJ are intoxicating the guests gathering around this corner.

126

中央部階段付近より1階の砂漠の風景画を配したパティオダイニングルーム（約70席）と2階カンクンルーム　トロピカルバー　レストランをみる
The patio dining room (about 70 seats) with a landscape of desert (1st floor) and the box room, tropical bar and restaurant (2nd floor), viewed from the central staircase area.

1階バーコーナー　夜の10時にＤＪが始まる頃は　このスペースも超満員になる　クリスタル製のイグアナの目の照明が一段とひきたつ
The 1st floor bar corner. At 10:00 p.m. when DJ begins, this space is jammed. The crystal iguana lighting stands out more impressively.

LUNCHEON SPECIALS

All menu items available during lunch

UN TACO

Chicken Ranchera	6.95
Steak Fajita	7.50

UNA ENCHILADA

Cheese	5.95
with chile con carne	6.95
Chicken Ranchera	7.95
Charbroiled Steak	8.50

BURGERS

Plain	5.95

1.00 for each additional topping
Jack cheese
Swiss cheese
Bacon
Cheddar cheese
Chili

TORTAS

Mexican sandwiches on toasted bolillos spread with guacamole and refried beans with melted jack cheese and grilled onions, with a choice of:

Charbroiled Chicken	7.25
Charbroiled Fajita Steak	7.95

Bowl of Chile and Salad	7.25
Pollo Taco Salad	9.50
Stuffed Avocado	9.95
Grilled Swordfish (6oz. lunch portion)	15.95

Luncheon specials available
Monday-Friday, 11:30AM-4PM

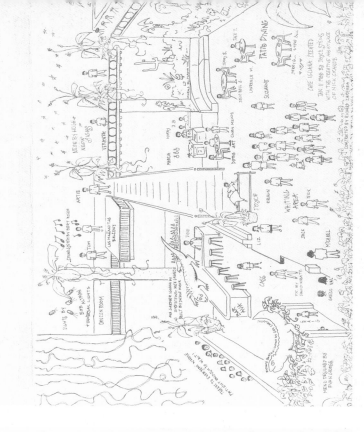

CAFE IGUANA

APPETIZERS

Tamales (2)
Corn masa filled with shredded chicken and vegetables, steamed in a corn husk, served with chile con carne and chile con queso. 6.75

Guacamole
Coarsely mashed avocado with cilantro, tomatoes, garlic and fresh lime juice. Season your order with the garnish tray. 5.50 Sm. 8.75 Lg.

Ceviche
Fresh fish of the day cooked by a marinade of lime juice and spices. 6.50

Shrimp Rellenos (2)
A spicy, pickled jalapeno filled with jack cheese and a jumbo shrimp, tossed in corn meal, flash fried, served with sour cream. 6.50

Chile Con Queso Dip
A soft blend of melted cheeses with pico de gallo, served with hot tortilla chips for dipping. 5.25

Tacquitos (3)
Shredded chicken in salsa ranchera, rolled tightly in a crispy corn tortilla, flash fried, served with sour cream and guacamole. 6.25

Artichoke En Vinaigrette
Steamed artichoke, served cold with mustard

Nachos

Cheese with a little jalapeno pepper melted over crispy corn chips, with choice of topping:

Cheese and Bean 4.95 Sm. 6.95 Lg.
Cheddar and jack cheese, refried beans.

Mixed cheeses 4.75 Sm. 6.75 Lg.
Cheddar and jack cheese.

Steak 6.75 Sm. 9.50 Lg.
Chunks of charbroiled fajita steak, cheddar cheese and guacamole.

Vegetable 5.25 Sm. 7.25 Lg.
Mushroom, bell pepper, onion and jack cheese.

Chicken 6.25 Sm. 8.75 Lg.
Chicken in salsa ranchera, jack cheese and sour cream.

SOUP

Consomme De Pollo Grande
Consomme with shredded chicken breast and avocado slices. Add the Mexican rice and pico de gallo for zestiness. 7.50

SALADS

Mixta Verde
Mixed, green salad with cumin vinaigrette dressing. 3.25

TEX-MEX SPECIALS

Served with Mexican rice, black beans and two flour tortillas.

Tacos

Soft, rolled flour tortilla sandwich with choice of:

Chicken 10.25
Charbroiled chicken with creamy sherry sauce.

Steak 12.25
Charbroiled fajita steak, served with chile con queso on the side.

Burrito Texano

Chicken in salsa ranchera, wrapped in one giant flour tortilla with refried beans and Mexican rice. 10.75

Enchiladas

Soft, corn tortilla wrapped around a filling, covered with gravy and topping, with choice of:

Cheddar Cheese 8.25
With cheddar cheese topping.

Cheddar Cheese 9.25
With cheddar cheese and chile con carne topping.

Chicken in Salsa Ranchera 10.25
With jack cheese and sour cream topping.

Charbroiled Fajita Steak 11.75
With cheddar cheese and chile con carne topping.

Vegetable 9.50
With jack cheese and sour cream topping.

Seafood in Salsa Ranchera 12.75
With jack cheese and sour cream topping.

FAJITA SPECIALS

Char-grilled meats, or chicken cut into strips, served on a sizzling platter, with Mexican rice and black beans. Roll your own tacos into two hand-rolled flour tortillas and spice them up from the garnish tray or with table sauces. Choice of:

	Chicken	Steak
Fajita Mexicana Topped with sauteed vegetables	14.50	15.75
Fajita Texana Plain	13.25	14.25
Fajita Fundido Topped with sauteed vegetables and melted cheese	15.75	17.25

GRILLED SPECIALS

Served with Mexican rice, black beans and two flour tortillas.

Charbroiled Swordfish Steak 19.50

Camarones Cancun 19.25
Jumbo shrimp, charbroiled in the shell, brushed with butter and lime, served on a sizzling platter.

Pechugas De Pollo 15.25
Boneless, skinless, charbroiled breast of chicken, served on a sizzling platter.

Alambre 15.95
Skewered, charbroiled fajita steak and jumbo shrimp, and vegetables.

Bistec Mexicano 19.50
Filet mignon, charbroiled.

Ranch Chicken 12.95
Half of a chicken, charbroiled.

The main dishes.

1／ステーキ トスタ―ダ
2／ステーキ ファジタメキシカ―ナ

ファサード　パシフィック　アベニーに面したコーナーに建つブリック造りの建物の1階
The facade. At the 1st floor of a brick building standing at a corner facing Pacific Ave.

オニックス材とユニークなドアのデザインを配したエントランス
The entrance with onyx and unique door design.

REBECCA'S

2025 Pacific Ave. Venice, CA 90028　Phone/213-306-6266

130

５ｍ以上もある２匹の鰐を空中に飾った客席　　　　　The guest seat area with two large crocodiles (longer than 5 m) in the air.

右側のダイニングエリアをみる

The dining area in the right side.

店内中央部のカウンターとバーコーナー
The central counter and bar corner.

レベッカ

建築デザイナーFrank Gehryを中心にアクアティック（水中）の風変わりなイメージを演出した「レベッカ」は　オーナーシェフのBruce Marder氏の提供する新しいスタイルのメキシコ料理とともに　いまロサンゼルスで最もホットなスポットとして話題になっている。19フィート（約5.7ｍ）もある鰐やジャイアント オクトパス（巨大な蛸）をダイニングエリアの天井部に泳がせたり　ベルベットの壁画やオニックスの板に後方より光をあてて壁面を浮き出さすなど　店内はまるで水中のファンタジィといった表現である。

「レベッカ」では　いままでのメキシコ料理のイメージを変え　食材や盛り付け　ボリュームなどまでも新しいスタイルに置き変えている。スープからサラダ　オードブルにサイドオーダーなどを約40種類メニューに加えて３～12ドルの幅で提供する　いわばグレージング感覚の料理と魚　チキン　牛肉などを使用し14～20ドルのアントレを22種類用意している。サンタモニカの南にあるこのベニス（Venice）地区には他にもユニークな店が増えておりモダンでリッチな雰囲気を求めてアーティストやヤッピーたちが集まって来ている。

オープンキッチンはバーコーナーの後方にあり　テーブル席より作業風景がみえる
The open kitchen is behind the bar corner, and cooking scenes are visible from the talbe seats.

開店／1986年5月5日
営業時間／6：00PM〜11：00PM（日〜木）
　　　　　6：00PM〜12：00AM（金・土）
客席数／160席
従業員数／70人

REBECCA'S

With the presentation of strange aquatic images hit on by Frank Gehry, architectural designer, etc., "REBECCA'S" is one of the hottest spots in Los Angeles, that offers new styles of Mexican dishes prepared by the owner-chef Bruce Marder.

A crocodile about 19 feet (5.7 m) long and a giant octopus are placed on the ceiling above the dining area. By casting light over the velvet frescos and onyx plates from behind them, the wall surface can stand out. Guests can feel thus as if they are surrounded by aquatic fantasy. Dishes at "Rebecca's" have changed the conventional images of Mexican dishes, and even materials, dishing up and volume acquired new styles. About 40 types of soup, salad, hors d'œuvre and side order are added to the menu, and served for a price of about $3 to 12. Using dishes that give a sense of "grazing," fish, chicken and beef, 22 types of entrée are offered for $14 to 20.
Other unique restaurants are also opening in this quarter (Venice) in the south of Santa Monica, being frequented by artists, yappies, etc. who are pursuing the modern, rich atmosphere.

Opened / May 5, 1986
Open /　6:00 p.m. to 11:00 p.m. (Sunday to Thursday)
　　　　6:00 p.m. to 12:00 a.m. (Friday · Saturday)
No. of guest seats /160
No. of employees / 70

水中のファンタジィを表現したベルベット地の壁面デザインとブース席
The velvet covered wall design expressing the underwater fantasy, and booth seat area.

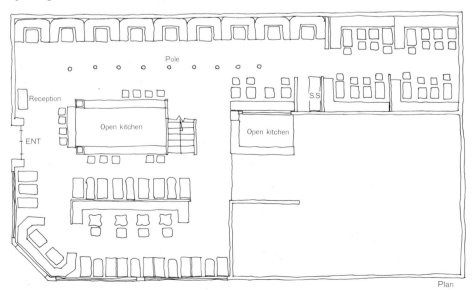

Plan

バック照明により浮き出て見えるオニックスの壁面も水中のイメージづくりのひとつだ
The onyx wall that stands out in relief due to the back lighting, is another setting for underwater image making.

①

②

③

主な料理

1/ Fried shrimp tacos.
2/ Duck rellend poblano.
3/ Charred squab Jalisco style

カウンター席をみる   The counter seats.

後方のジャイアント オクトパス（巨大な蛸）を配した客席の雰囲気は異様な感じを与える
The guest seat area with a giant octopus behind, gives a strange impression.

136

シャイアント オクトパス   The giant octopus.

蛸の泳ぐダイニングエリア   The dining area where an octopus is swimming.

静寂感がまだ残っているトライベッカ地区への出店店舗（左側1階） 後方にワールド トレードレセンターが見える
The restaurant (left side, 1st floor) opened in Tribecca area where quietness remains. Visible behind is the World Trace Center.

323 Greenwich St. New York, N.Y. 10013
Phone/212-334-9190

倉庫を改装したレストランのファサードとネオンサイン
The facade and neon sign of the restaurant that has come
into being by redecorating a warehouse.

138

アイドルタイムにも予約の電話が鳴り　連日賑わっている
Even during idle time the telephone keeps ringing for reservation. The restaurant is crowded with guests everyday.

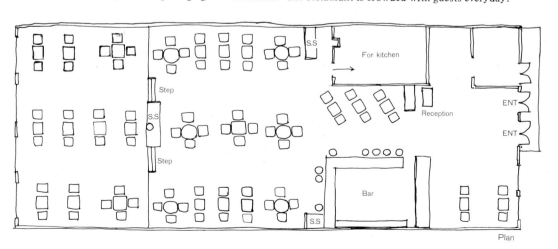

S.S

For kitchen

Step

ENT

S.S

Reception

ENT

Step

Bar

S.S

Plan

139

上／アートギャラリーの雰囲気で 天井空間の高い客席はファッションやミュージック関係 ヤッピーたちに人気がある
左下／自家製ケーキのショーケースを前面に置き バーカウンターをその後方に配置している
Top / With an atmosphere of art gallery, the guest seat area under a high ceiling in patronized by people involved in fashion, music, etc., and by yappies.
Left, bottom / The homemade confectionery showcase is placed in your side, and bar counter behind.

トミー タン

エスニック料理の感心が高いアメリカでは メキシコ料理などと共に 最近では ベトナムやタイ 中国 韓国といったアジア地域の料理が注目されている。この店はバンコック生まれのオーナー シェフであるトミー タンの斬新な味つけと芸術的な盛りつけで人気のタイ レストランである。1970年に渡米して以来 音楽関係の仕事をはじめ幾多の職業を変えながら 最後に到達したのがレストランの世界である。長年アメリカに住みアメリカ人の好みを知ることにより 彼の感性とうまく組合った彼独自の料理は地元ロサンゼルス タイムス紙をはじめ多くのマスコミに紹介され評判を呼ぶまでにはそう時間がかからなかった。一躍有名になった彼は約2年後にニューヨークの2号店を持つに至ったのである。西海岸と東海岸の大都市に店を持ったシェフとしては稀な成功者といえる。妻のSandiは店の運営を中心に動き タイから呼び寄せたトミーの家族や親戚の人たちがキッチンを助けている。

開店／1986年10月27日
営業時間／11:30AM～ 3:00PM（ランチ：月～金）

90席のダイニングエリアは後方に一段高くしたコーナーを設け　見通しの良い構成にしている
The dining area with 90 seats is arranged at a level a little higher than the surrounding area, so that guests can have an unobstructed view.

6：00PM～11：30PM（ディナー：月～金）
6：00PM～12：00AM（ディナー：金・土）
休日／日曜・祭日
客席数／90席（ダイニングエリア）　10席（バー）
従業員数／35人
客単価／ランチ　20ドル
　　　　ディナー　35ドル

TOMMY TANG'S

In America where people are very interested in ethnic dishes, people's interest is currently shifting to Asian dishes (Vietnamese, Thai, Chinese, Korean, etc.), in addition to Mexican dishes. This Thai restaurant is popular for the owner-chef Tommy Tang's (born in Bangkok) unique seasoning and artistic dishing up.

Since he went over to the U.S. in 1970, he has experiences in various professions, including music related activities, and has finally come into the world of restaurants. Through living in the U.S. for many years, he has deeply grasped the American taste, and his own dishes based on his unique sensitivity have been reported by Los Angeles Times (local paper), and many other mass communication media. So, it has not been long before his dishes became famous. With his success, he could open the 2nd restaurant in New York two years later. With his restaurants in West Coast and East Coast, he represents a rare case of successful chef. His wife Sandi is mainly undertaking the operations, and Tommy's family and relatives are helping in the kitchen.

Opened / October 27, 1986
Open / 11:30 a.m. to 3:00 p.m. (lunch: Monday to Friday)
　　　6:00 p.m. to 11:30 p.m. (dinner: Monday to Friday)
　　　6:00 p.m. to 12:00 a.m. (dinner: Friday · Saturday)
Closed / Sunday · holiday
No. of guest seats / 90 (dining area),　10 (bar)
No. of employees / 35
Price per guest / lunch: $20,　dinner: $35

アートギャラリーの雰囲気をもつ店内　壁面の作品は定期的にアーチストによって持込まれる
The inside with an atmosphere of art gallery. The pieces of artistic work on the wall are brought in by artists.

①

②

③

主な料理

1/ Lemon grass chicken.
2/ Grilled tuna steak.
3/ Original Tommy duck.

上・左／1階バー（52席）にはSandro chia氏が描いたイタリアのパリオ地方のホースレースのイベント風景の絵画が
上部壁面いっぱいに飾られ圧巻である　その下にはマーブルのバーカウンターが配されている

左上・右上／新しく建った「Equitable Center」の中央部に出店したファサード
Left, top · right, top / The facade of the restaurant opened in the newly built "Equitable Center."

PALIO

151 West 51 St. New York, N.Y. 10019　Phone/212-245-4850

Left, top · top / At the 1st floor bar (52 seats), the picture of a horse race event scene in Palio district, Italy, is fully painted over the upper part of the wall, giving a dramatic impression. Below it is the marble bar counter.

パリオ

"フランス料理の源流はイタリア料理だ"といわれる
くらい 古い歴史を持つイタリア料理であるが イ
タリア本国ではいま格調ある本格的な料理の復興が
始まっているといわれる。

イタリア出身でニューヨークに「La Camelia」と
「Sandro's」というイタリア料理店を持つ この店の
経営者Tomy May氏は そのような本国の新しい
波をいち早く受けとめ「パリオ」を開店した。

シェフのAndreada Merano氏は30年の料理経験か
ら 経営者の意をくみ 現在のアメリカ人のライフ
スタイルに合ったイタリア料理を追求している。店
舗のデザインはMassimo Vignelli氏で食器からメ
ニュー ユニフォームまで手掛けている。1階バーの壁
画はSandro Chia氏の作品。

開店／1987年3月

営業時間／12:00PM～ 2:00AM（ランチ：月～金）
　　　　　5:30PM～11:00PM（ディナー：月～土）
　　　　　11:30AM～12:00AM（バー：月～金）
　　　　　4:00PM～12:00AM（バー：土）

客席数／125席（レストラン）52席（バー）40席（プラ
　　　　イベートルーム：2室）

従業員数／90～100人

客単価／ランチ20～28ドル ランチ定食32.50ドル
　　　　ディナー22～35ドル

PALIO

Italian dishes have such a long history that it is
said that "French dishes have originated from
Italian dishes." Presently traditional dishes are
becoming popular in Italy.

Tomy May from Italy, owner of Italian restaurants "La Camelia" and "Sandro's" in New York,
has opened "Pario," swiftly catching the new
wave in his home country.

Fully grasping the owner's intention, the chef,
Andreada Merano, is preparing Italian dishes that
blend well with the current American life style,
based on his 30 years cooking experience. The
shop design has been undertaken by Massimo
Vignelli, from the tableware to menu and even
the waiters' uniform. The fresco at the 1st floor
bar corner has been painted by Sandro Chia.

Opened / March 1987
Open /　12:00 p.m. to 2:00 a.m.
　　　　　　(lunch: Monday to Friday)
　　　　5:30 p.m. to 11:00 p.m.
　　　　　　(dinner: Monday to Saturday)
　　　　11:30 a.m. to 12:00 a.m.
　　　　　　(bar: Monday to Friday)
　　　　4:00 p.m. to 12:00 a.m.
　　　　　　(bar: Saturday)
No. of guest seats /　125 (restaurant),　52 (bar),
　　　　　　　　　　40 (private room: 2)
No. of employees /　90 to 100
Price per guest /　lunch: $20 to 28,
　　　　　　　　　lunch (table d'hôte): $32.50
　　　　　　　　　dinner: $22 to 35

2階ダイニングへ通じる専用エレベーターのホールとレセプション
The hall of the special elevator leading to the 2nd floor dining area, and the reception.

同店のデザインはMassima Vignelli氏により食器からメニュー ユニホームにいたるまで手がけられている
The restaurant's design is undertaken by Massimo Vignelli covering tableware, menu and even uniform.

2階にあるレストラン全景（125席）をみる　全体は3つのセクションに分けられている
The entire scene of the restaurant (125 seats) at the 2nd floor. It is partitioned into three sections.

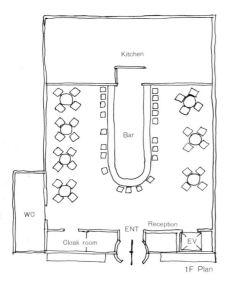

1F Plan

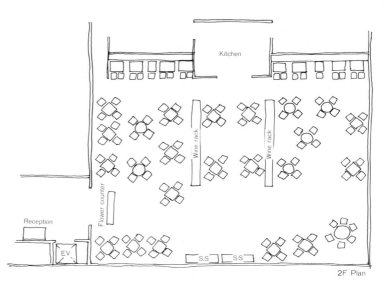

2F Plan

ワインラックで 3 つのセクションに仕切られた 2 階ダイニングエリア　広い空間を感じさせる
The 2nd floor dining area partitioned into three sections by wine racks, giving a spacious impression.

①

②

③

ホースレースに集まった由緒ある旗が2階のダイニングルームの壁面を飾る
The time-honored flags gathered to horse races decorate the wall of the 2nd floor dining room.

1／マグロのタルタルと茄子のマリネ　バジルソース
2／ミラノ風オッソブコ（Ossobuco）
3／サーモンのロール巻き

The main dishes.

エレガントなテーブルセッティングの演出もこのレストランの特徴
The elegant presentation of table setting is another feature of this restaurant.

ファサード

The facade.

10506 Santa Monica Blvd. Los Angeles, CA. 90025
Phone/213-470-8446

フレッシュな花が印象的な店内 　　The inside scene impressive with fresh flowers.

ダイニングルームの中央より絵画の飾られた壁面をみる　　　　　The wall decorated with pictures, viewed from the center of the dining room.

シャンペン

シャンペンの泡が立ち上るロゴマークの新しいフレンチ・カリフォルニア料理店である。若いオーナーシェフのPatrick Healy は「ムーラン ド ムージャン」のロジェ ヴェルジュをはじめトロワグロ ミシェル ゲラルドなど師事した5年間のフランスにおける修業が今日の成功につながっている。週末の予約は何週間か先でなくてはとれないほどであり　ロサンゼルスのレストランの中でもホットな話題となっている店である。フランス人の奥さんがマネージャーを兼ね　二人三脚の営業も親しまれている。料理にはコンテンポラリー スパクラシックおよびラスティック（田舎風）とバラエティに富むメニューを用意しているのも特徴。センチュリーシティの西側に位置する住宅地のロケーションは決して良くないがこれらの新しい料理と若さを感じさせる店のサービス コンテンポラリーな絵画　花をアクセントにしたテーブルセッティング　シンプルな店内装飾がユニークさを強調している。

開店／1987年10月14日
営業時間／11：00AM〜 2：30PM（ランチ：火〜金）
　　　　　6：00PM〜10：30PM（ディナー：火〜日）
休日／月曜日　客席数／100席　従葉員数／30人
客単価／ランチ20ドル　ディナー55ドル

CHAMPAGNE

A new French-Californian restaurant featuring a logo mark of champagne bubbling up. The young owner-chef Patrick Healy had trained himself for five years in France, under Loje Velju of Le Moulin de Mougins, Michel Gerald of Troisgros, etc. Week-end reservation must be made several weeks in advance. This is really one of the hottest spots in Los Angeles. His French wife is serving as a manager, and this couple is another reason of popularity.

The menu contains a variety of dishes from contemporary to super-classic and rustic. Although the restaurant is not necessarily located favorably (in a residential quarter of the western side of Century City), its new dishes, service giving a young, fresh sense, contemporary paintings, table setting accented with flowers and simple décor are stressing its uniqueness.

Opened / October 14, 1987
Open /　11:00 a.m. to 2:30 p.m. (lunch: Tuesday to Friday)
　　　　6:00 p.m. to 10:30 p.m. (dinner: Tuesday to Sunday)
Closed / Monday
No. of guest seats / 100
No. of employees / 30
Price per guest / lunch: $20,　dinner: $55

シャンペンの泡を配したサインボードと石壁に小窓を設けたファサード　黄色のテントがポイント
The signboard with champagne bubbles, and the facade of stone wall with small windows, accented with a yellow tent.

フランスの三つ星レストラン「ムーラン　ド　ムージャン」を模して造った店内
The inside designed by modeling after "Moulin d'Moujan," a three-star restaurant in France.

大きな窓を設けた明るい店内(100席)

窓側よりみる　右側にもう一つの部屋がある　　　　　　A scene viewed from the window side. Another room is in the right side.

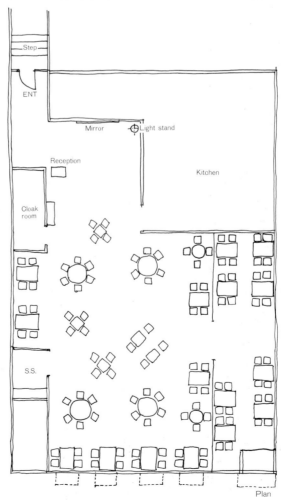

広いダイニングルームの中央部をみる　　　　　　The central part of the wide dining area.

Step

ENT

Mirror　Light stand

Reception

Cloak room

Kitchen

S.S.

Plan

①

②

③

1／クレイフィッシュと大茄子のケイク
2／カリカリしたノルウェー産のサーモン
3／チョコレートのシャルロット　ラズベリーソース

The main dishes.

左／花とコンテンポラリーな絵画やデコアがアクセントとなっている店内
Left / The inside accented with contemporary pictures and décor.

モダンアートデコのファサード

The facade in modern art deco design.

CITY GRILL

Los Angeles Hilton & Towers 930 Wilshire Blvd. Los Angeles, CA 90017 Phone/213-623-5971

レセプション近くの円形テーブルのある客席
The guest seat area with a round table near the reception.

円形バーを中心に展開するテーブル席は　ランチのあとカクテルラウンジに開放している
The table seat area centering around the round bar is opened as a cocktail lounge, after lunch service.

円形バーカウンターに合わせたダイニングエリアのレイアウト

The layout of the dining area set according to the round bar counter.

テーマカラーでもある海面の緑を思わせるナプキンを配したバンケットルームよりダイニングをみる
The dining room viewed from the banquet room where napkins in sea surface green color — theme color — are arranged.

奥のメインダイニングルームと開放的でエレガントなバンケットルーム
The inner main dining room and open, elegant banquet room.

入口を入ると長いバーカウンターが右側にあり　奥は円形カウンターになっている
Entering the restaurant the long bar counter is set in the right side, and the round counter is placed inside.

シティ グリル

ロサンゼルスのダウンタウンにある「ヒルトン ＆ タワーズ ホテル」は
かつてのステーキレストランであった「ビーフ バロン」を改装し　ラン
チを主体としたこのレストランを1987年夏にオープンした。
海面のような緑と灰色がかったバラ色をテーマカラーとした店内は　明
るい広々としたモダンアートデコのエレガントな雰囲気となっている。
料理はアイテムをしぼり　スペシャルメニューに人気のある料理や季節
感のある料理を加えている。
ランチタイムのあとはタパス料理をオードブルとして提供するカクテル
ラウンジに変化し　午後7時まで開放するという完全にビジネス客を対
象としており　ディナーの営業はない。

開店／1987年 7 月15日
営業時間／11:30AM〜2:00PM（ランチ）
　　　　　2:00PM〜7:00PM（カクテル）
客席数／147席　従業員数／19人　客単価／12ドル

CITY GRILL

"Hilton & Towers Hotel" downtown Los Angeles brought this restaurant (mainly serving lunch) into being in the summer of 1987 by
redecorating the former steak restaurant "Beef Baron."
The inside whose theme is green like sea surface and greyish rose
color, gives an elegant atmosphere of bright, spacious, modern art
deco. The menu items are selected, including special items that
either popular or seasonal.
After the lunch time, the restaurant changes into a cocktail lounge
serving tapas dishes as hors d'œuvre, and is opened to guests by
7:00 p.m.. Thus, fully intended to business guests, this restaurants
offers no dinner service.

Opened / July 15, 1987
Open /　11:30 a.m. to 2:00 p.m. (lunch)
　　　　2:00 p.m. to 7:00 p.m. (cocktail)
No. of guest seats / 147
No. of employees / 19
Price per guest / $12

円形ベンチシートより円形カウンターをみる

The round counter viewed from the round bench seat

メインダイニングをみる　The main dining room.

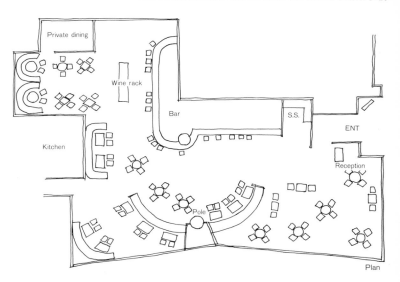

Plan

店内に設置されたワインカラーと奥のメインダイニングルーム
The wine cellar installed inside, and the inner main dining.

ケイジャンチキンサラダ　スパイシーホットペッパー添え

フレッシュ　サンタバーバラシュリンプバターソースかけ

The main dishes.

左／円形カウンターをみる　アフターランチはバーラウンジとしてタパスのオードブルを提供するという新しいコンセプト

Left / The round counter. After the lunch, it serves as a bar lounge offering tapas hors d'œuvre – a new concept.

3rdアベニューと40丁目の交差点のオフィスビル1階に出店した2号店のファサード
The facade of the 2nd shop opened at the 1st floor of an office building standing at a crossing of 3rd Avenue and 40th street.

DOCKS
OYSTER BAR & SEAFOOD GRILL

633 3rd Ave. New York, N.Y. 10017
Phone/212-986-8080

ダイニングエリアより入口とレセプション方向をみる

The entrance and reception area viewed from the dining area.

中2階より275席という広いダイニングエリアをみる

The wide dining area with 275 seats viewed from the mezzanine.

奥のオイスターバーと2階のトイレを結ぶ階段をみる　壁にはデイリースペシャルのメニューが書き込まれている
The staircase connecting the inner oyster bar and toilet at the 2nd floor. The daily specials menu is written on the wall.

シェフ Ellis Simberioff 氏は"常に鮮度をチェックし　できるだけ安価に提供できる料理がモットーだ"という
The chef, Ellis Simberioff, makes it his motto to "always check the freshness and offer as cheap dishes as possible."

169

ダイニングエリアよりバーカウンターをみる　マホガニー製の棚が格調を高めている
The bar counter viewed from the dining area. The mahogany shelves help in giving a dignified atmosphere.

ドックス

ニューヨークにはシーフードを楽しめるレストランが多い。シーズンともなると　大小様々な形のオイスターやクラムなどのフレッシュな魚介類が味わえる。
「ドックス」はウエストサイドのブロードウェイ89番街の1号店に次いでの2号店である。1号店は　カジュアルで比較的安価に食事が出来る店として　穴場的存在であり　その成功が　今回イーストサイドのグランド　セントラル駅の近くに2号店の出店を可能にしたというわけだ。
275席という大きなスペースを持ち　オフィスと住宅(コンドミニアム)を背景にした好立地にあり1日平均総来客数800人を越えるという盛況ぶりである。

開店／1988年8月16日
営業時間／11:30AM～ 3:00PM (ランチ：月～土)
　　　　　5:00PM～11:30PM (ディナー：月～土)
　　　　　9:00AM～ 4:00PM (ブランチ：日)
　　　　　5:00PM～11:00PM (ディナー：日)
客席数／275席
従業員数／120人(内サービス60人　キッチン60人)
客単価／ランチ25ドル　ディナー30ドル(飲物含む)

DOCKS

There are many restaurants where guests can enjoy seafoods. During the season, fresh fish, such as oysters and clams varying in size, are served.
Following the first "Docks" at Street 89, Broadway, this is the second "Docks." The first restaurant is a nice spot for guests who wish to enjoy casual dishes at relatively moderate prices. This success has paved the way for opening the second restaurant near the Grand Central Station, East Side.
With a large space and 275 seats, it is favorably surrounded by offices and condominiums, and is frequented by more than 800 guests/day on the overage.

Opened / August 16, 1988
Open /　11:30 a.m. to 3:00 p.m. (lunch: Monday to Saturday)
　　　　5:00 p.m. to 11:30 p.m. (dinner: Monday to Saturday)
　　　　9:00 a.m. to 4:00 p.m. (brunch: Sunday)
　　　　5:00 p.m. to 11:00 p.m. (dinner: Sunday)
No. of guest seats / 275
No. of employees / 120 (service: 60,　kitchen: 60)
Price per guest / lunch: $25,　dinner: $30 (incl. drinks)

レセプション廻りに展開するバーエリアとダイニングテーブル

The bar area and dining table developed around the reception area.

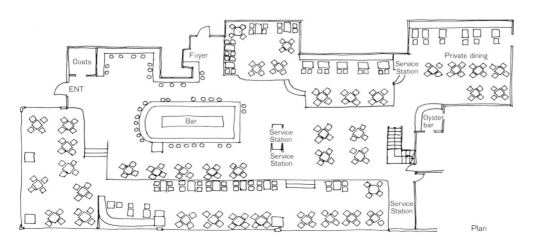

Plan

ロブスターとオイスター　レッドクラムソースのリングィーニ

オイスター類とシュリンプ　ロブスターの盛合せ

The main dishes.

左／入口近くのバーカウンターに設けられた新鮮な魚介類のディスプレイとランチタイムに利用するテーブルセット

Left / The display of fresh fish provided at the bar counter near the entrance, and the table set used at lunch time.

明るいカリブ ブルーを配したファサード

The facade featuring the bright Caribbean blue.

Cha Cha Cha

656 N. Virgil Ave. Los Angeles, CA 90004
Phone/213-664-7723

開放的な入口あたりのレセプションにはアンティークの時計 ユニークなデザインのス
ツールが置かれている
At the reception near the open entrance are placed an antique clock and
uniquely designed stool.

カリブの香りを感じさせる店内　壁面と天井　テーブルクロスや壁面の絵の色まてコーディネイトし　生花てアクセントをつけている
The inside with a Caribbean fragrance. The colors of the wall, ceiling, table cloth and even pictures on the wall are coordinated, and accented with fresh flowers.

チャ チャ チャ

エスニックブームのアメリカのレストラン界にカリブ料理レストランが登場　話題になっている。太平洋に面したロサンゼルスにカリブ海地方の料理がやって来たというわけであるが　開店以来多くの客で賑わっている。

ユニークなレストランやブティックの並ぶメルローズ通りの東のはずれに近い一角にカリブブルーとでも表現するような　明るい青空の色を配したファサードが一段と目につく。オーナーのMario Tamayo氏は元はヘアースタイリストであったが　店づくりのアイデアはもとより料理のプレゼンテーションも彼が中心となって出来上がった。店内は壁や天井の色にテーブルクロス　壁面の絵の色までコーディネートし　生花でアクセントをつけ　カリブの香りを感じさせている。

開店／1986年6月14日
営業時間／11:30AM～ 3:00PM（ランチ：月～土）
　　　　　　6:00PM～11:00PM（ディナー：月～土）
　　　　　　5:00PM～11:00PM（ディナー：日）
客席数／49席　25席（パティオ）
従業員数／23人

CHA CHA CHA

In the midst of the ongoing ethnic boom of American restaurant business, this Caribbean restaurant has been established with great success. Dishes from the Caribbean Sea have come in Los Angeles facing the Pacific Ocean. Since its opening, "Cha Cha Cha" has been patronized by many people.

At a corner near the eastern end of Melrose Avenue where there stand unique restaurants and boutiques, the facade in bright sky blue, that recalls the Caribbean blue, is even more attractive. The owner, Mario Tamayo, was a former hair stylist, but he has played the central role not merely in shop making but also in the presentation of dishes. The colors of wall and ceiling of the restaurant, as well as the table cloth or pictures on the wall, are coordinated, with beautiful fresh flowers that give the typical Caribbean flavor.

Opened / June 14, 1986
Open / 11:30 a.m. to 3:00 p.m. (lunch: Monday to Saturday)
　　　　6:00 p.m. to 11:00 p.m. (dinner: Monday to Saturday)
　　　　5:00 p.m. to 11:00 p.m. (dinner: Sunday)
No. of guest seats / 49, 25 (patio)
No. of employees / 23

①

②

③

主な料理

1/ Cucumber and Fennel, Yogurt dressing
2/ Tomato y Basilico
3/ Cha Cha Chicken

左／カリブの風と太陽がそのまま店内に入ってくるような開放的雰囲気の店内

Left / The inside atmosphere is such that you may feel as if the Caribbean wind
      and sunlight enter into the restaurant.

177

壁面の絵はギャラリーも経営するマリオ氏のコレクションや友人のアーティストの作品を定期的に入れ替える
The pictures on the wall are periodically replaced by selecting from the collection of Mr. Mario who is managing a gallery, and pictures painted by artists who are his friends.

25席のパティオ ダイニングは南国のムードを楽しめるコーナー
The patio dining with 25 seats is a corner where guests can enjoy the mood of a southern country.

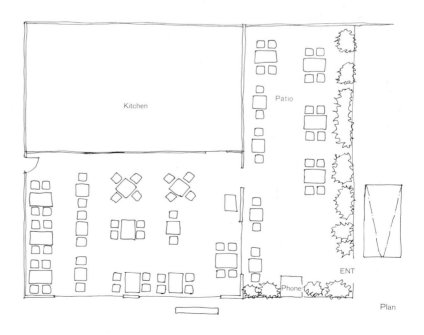

Kitchen

Patio

ENT

Phone

Plan

ユニオンスクエアからも近い O'farrell 通りに面したレストランのファサード
The facade of the restaurant facing O'farrell Street which is near Union Square.

細長いバーカウンターは入口近くにあり　ワインのグラス売りにも力を入れ　壁面中央に
黒板を用いて手書きの表示もしている
The narrow bar counter is close to the entrance, and glass sales of wine are actively promoted. Handwritten information is also given on the blackboard in the wall center.

242 O'farrell St. San Francisco, CA 94102
Phone/415-982-9353

180

軽快なジャズ音楽はバーラウンジに置かれたスタインウエイのピアノでディナータイムと日曜日の夕方のみ演奏する
Cheerful jazz is performed only at dinner time and in Sunday evening by Steinway's piano placed at the bar lounge.

壁際のテーブル席は映画や観劇の前後の食事を楽しむカップルの客が好んで座る
The table seats by the wall are often occupied by couples who wish to enjoy eating before or after cinema- or theater-going.

ジルス

サンフランシスコは全米の大都市の中で　最もレストランの競合がはげ
しいといわれている所であり1店あたり158世帯が対象という統計がある
くらいだ。あえてこの場所を選んでレストラン経営に挑んだ3人の若い
（全員26歳）共同経営者たちの店である。彼等は他にもいくつかの共通点
を持っているのもユニークだ。全員がオランダ人であり　ハーグにある
ホテル　レストランの専門学校に学び　後にヨーロッパとアメリカの一流
レストランやホテルでマネージメントとサービス　料理のそれぞれの分野
で活躍した経験を活かしてこの店を開店した。店名は3人のファースト
ネームの頭文字を組み合わせてつけたものである。国際都市サンフラン
シスコにヨーロッパとアメリカの新しい息吹が注ぎこまれ　若い3人の
斬新なアイデアによるレストランがスタートした。このような姿がこれ
からもアメリカ中に多くみられるにちがいない。

開店／1987年2月7日
営業時間／11:30AM〜 3:00PM（ランチ：月〜土）
　　　　　 5:00PM〜11:00PM（ディナー：月〜土）
　　　　　 5:00PM〜10:00PM（ディナー：日）
　　　　　 5:00PM〜 8:30PM（ライブジャズ：日）
客席数／130席（レストラン）　30席（バー）
従業員数／20人

JIL'S

San Francisco is a big city in the U.S. where restaurants are competing fiercely among them. There even is a statistical fact that the territory of one restaurant includes only 158 families. "JIL'S" is a restaurant managed jointly by three young owners (26 years old) who have challenged operation in this competitive city. It is also unique that they have several points in common. All of them are Dutch, have been trained at a professional school on hotels & restaurants in Hague, and later worked at leading restaurants and hotels in Europe and America, specializing in management, service and cooking, respectively. The shop name comes from a combination of the initial letters of the three owners' first names.
With an innovative restaurant concept created by the three young owners, a new restaurant filled with fresh European and American atmosphere opened in San Francisco, an international city. Many new styles of restaurant like "JIL'S" will appear here and there in America.

Opened / February 7, 1987
Open /　11:30 p.m. to 3:00 p.m. (lunch: Monday to Saturday)
　　　　5:00 p.m. to 11:00 p.m. (dinner: Monday to Saturday)
　　　　5:00 p.m. to 10:00 p.m. (dinner: Sunday)
　　　　5:00 p.m. to 8:30 p.m. (live jazz: Sunday)
No. of guest seats / 130 (restaurant), 30 (bar)
No. of employees / 20

ダイニングルームの中央にあるタイル貼りの柱をアクセントにしている

Accented with the tiled pillar in the center of the dining room.

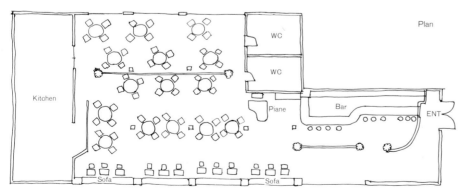

Plan

Kitchen

WC

WC

Piane

Bar

ENT

Sofa

Sofa

スポットライトを生かした店内の演出
The inside presentation effectively utilizing the spotlight.

ヨーロッパとアメリカの感覚を持ち込み　新しいビストロのスタイルを演出したダイニングルーム
The dining room presented as a new-style bistro by introducing both European and American senses.

ヨーロッパ出身の若いアーチストたちの現代風の作品が飾られ 若い経営者たちの感覚がここにも表現されている

Top / The senses of young managers are also expressed here, as contemporary works of young artists from Europe are displayed.

主な料理

1/ Terrine of asparagus
2/ Salmon cakes with asparagus
3/ Grand dessert Jil's

2階建て木造オフィスを改造し　ネオンサインをつけたモダンな装いのエントランス廻り
The entrance area in modern appearance with neon sign, brought into being by a wooden two-storied office building.

Curry
Club

6623 Melrose Ave. Los Angeles, CA 90038
Phone/213-939-2018

ファサード

The facade.

クリーンなイメージを出した白を強調するオープンキッチンとカウンター席（7席）をみる
The open kitchen and counter seats (7) emphasizing "white" to give a clean image.

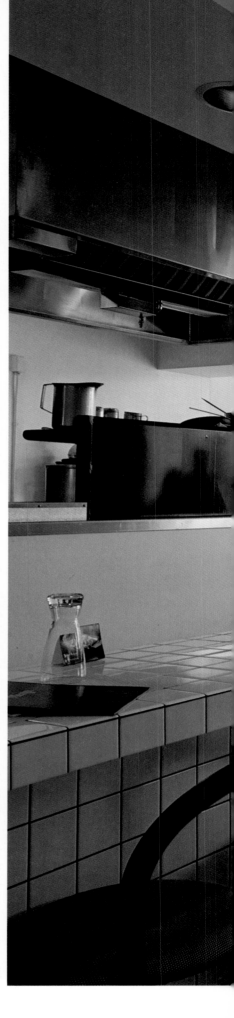

ローカルのアーチストによる作品を壁面に展示したテーブル席
The table seats by the wall on which works of local artists are displayed.

カウンター席うしろの壁面中央部に大きな窓を設け　アートギャラリーが見えるように演出
By securing a large window in the center of the wall behind the counter seats, an art gallery is made visible.

店内奥よりカウンター席　オープンキッチン　入口方向をみる　　　　The counter seats, open kitchen and entrance area viewed from an inner part.

店内前面部中央にもギャラリー風の雰囲気を出している　　　　　The central part of the front side is also arranged to give a gallery-like atmosphere.

カレー クラブ

カレー料理といえばインドの料理と思うのはアメリカ人も同様であるが
日本式カレー料理というので　話題になっているレストランがここ。
ロサンゼルスのメルロース通りに立地しているが　アンティークショッ
プやレストランの並んだ一角より少し離れたところに出店していて　ロ
スで最もホットなレストランのひとつに数えられる「CITRUS」(本書76
ページ収録)のとなりにある。出店したのは日本人である。店内はまる
でアートギャラリーを思わせる複合ショップで　ローカルのアーチスト
たちの絵画や焼き物 家具 アクセサリーといった作品の展示 販売コー
ナーとダイニングエリアとで構成されている。
メニューは日本式カレーライスが　メインのアントレとして6種類ある。
野菜のミックス カレー マッシュルーム カレー ビーフ チキン シュ
リンプと帆立てカレーなどであり　価格は3ドル50セントまで。カレー
にはサフランライスと新鮮なサラダ ピクルス類がつく。その他サーモン
のソテー 海老のコロッケなども人気が高い。
開店／1988年3月1日
営業時間／11：30AM〜 9：00PM(月〜木)
　　　　　 11：30AM〜10：00PM(金)

　　　　　 2：00PM〜10：00PM(土)
休日／日躍日　客席数／24席
従業員数／7人　客単価／6.15ドル

CURRY CLUB

As in other countries, Americans also think that curry dishes and
synonymous with Indian dishes. This restaurant is drawing attention,
since it offers Japanese-style curry dishes.
Though it stands at Melrose Avenue, Los Angeles, it is a little away
from the area crowded with antique shops and restaurants – next
to "Citrus" (that appears on page 76 of this book) that is one of
the most popular restaurants in Los Angeles. It has been opened
by a Japanese. A composite shop that reminds us of an art gallery,
the inside is composed of a display/sales corner for pictures, ceramic
ware, furniture, accessories, etc. produced by local artists, and a
dining area.

アメリカ人による日本的な作品を中心に集めた販売コーナーも併設している
The selling corner, where Japanese-style works of Americans are displayed, is also provided.

The menu comprises six items of Japanese curry rice as the main entrée – that is, curry mixed with vegetables, mushroom, beef, chicken, shrimp and scallop curries whose prices are up to $3.50. Each curry comes with saffron rice, fresh salad and pickles. Salmon sauté, shrimp croquette, etc. are also very popular.

Opened / March 1, 1988
Open / 11:30 a.m. to 9:00 p.m. (Monday to Thursday)
        11:30 a.m. to 10:00 p.m. (Friday)
        2:00 p.m. to 10:00 p.m. (Saturday)
Closed / Sunday
No. of guest seats / 24
No. of employees / 7
Price per guest / $6.15

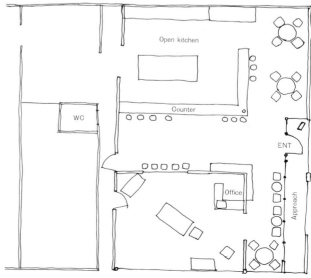

Plan

自然光が入る明るいダイニングエリアとその周囲に展示された作品　The bright dining area where natural light enters, and works of art displayed around it.

アートギャラリーを併設したコーナーの窓からカウンターとオープンキッチンがみえる
The counter and open kitchen viewed from the corner's window provided with the art gallery.

左/ビーフカレー（サフランライスとサラダ　ピクルス付き）とサーモンソテー　クリーム　ド　シュリンプコロッケ

The main dishes.

45番街とレキシントン通りの交差点角に出店し成功した第一号店
The 1st shop successfully opened at a corner of the crossing of 45th street and Lexington Avenue.

LE CROISSANT SHOP®

459 Lexington Ave. New York, N.Y. 10017
Phone/212-697-5580

Right / In the left side of the front entrance is a special entrance for soup takeout.

正面入口左側にはスープのテイクアウト専用の入口を設けている

狭い店内は常時あふれるようにベーカリー商品を置いている　忙しい時には2列に並んだラインで客にサービスする
In the narrow space bakery is always placed abundantly.　When crowded, the staffs respond to guests in two rows.

道路に面した細い力ウンターでは簡単な食事もできる

At the narrow counter facing the road, simple meal can be taken.

バラエティのあるサラダやサンドイッチ類の具材を用いるフレッシュなアイテムを並べる冷蔵ショーケース 客は好みのサンドイッチを組み立てオーダーする
A cold storage showcase displaying fresh items using a variety of salads and sandwiches. Guests order them in a combination they prefer.

クロワッサンの種類は10種類以上 このメニューはクロワッサンのデイルチキンサンドイッチ 青豆のポタージュスープ シェフサラダ
Croissant is available in more than ten types. This menu is a set of dill chicken sandwich of croissant, green beans potage soup and chef salad.

ル クロワッサン ショップ

1980年代の初期に始まったクロワッサンブームの火付け役のひとつがこの「ル ク
ロワッサン ショップ」である。1号店であるこの店は 1981年5月にオープンし
た。
フランス生まれのオーナーの Robert Le Lamar 氏と彼の奥さん そしてペイスト
リーシェフ Pierre Bosc 氏によるチームワークが見事に実り1日に2,000個もの
クロワッサンを売ったという記録をもっている。フランスの香りとアメリカ人の
好む味がぴったり一致したクロワッサンは ニューヨークやサンフランシスコな
ど大都市から全米へと広がり 非常に人気のあるパンとしてすっかり定着してい
る。
「ル クロワッサン ショップ」はニューヨークを中心にアメリカ イスラエル 日
本などにフランチャイズ方式で店舗展開を進めている。
開店／1981年5月
営業時間／6:30AM～7:00PM(月～金)
　　　　　8:00AM～6:00PM(土)
　　　　　8:30AM～4:30PM(日)

LE CROISSANT SHOP

One of the pioneers of the croissant boom that took place early in the 1980's,
is this "Le Croissant Shop." Opened in May 1981, this is the first shop in the
chain.
Due to the wonderful teamwork by the French born owner Robert Le Lamar,
his wife, and the pastry chef Pierre Bosc, they have achieved amazing sales —
once sold 2,000 pieces of croissant. Being an ideal embodiment of French flavor
and American taste, croissants have spread from big cities, such as New York
and San Francisco, to all over the U.S., and have firm root in the American taste
as a very popular bread.
"Le Croissant Shop" is developing its chain under the franchise system, from
New York in the main to Israel, Japan, etc.

Opened / May 1981
Open / 6:30 a.m. to 7:00 p.m. (Monday to Friday)
　　　　8:00 a.m. to 6:00 p.m. (Saturday)
　　　　8:30 a.m. to 4:30 p.m. (Sunday)

左／商品ケースと奥にはフレッシュなパンを焼くオーブンが配置されている
Left / The showcase, and an oven for baking fresh bread placed at an inner part.

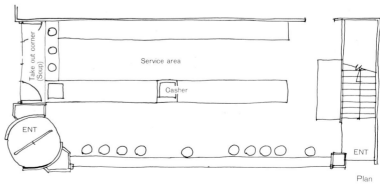

Plan

バーコーナーではワインの特別銘柄のグラス売りやビールの販促にも積極的
The bar corner is positively making glass sales of special brand wine, and beer sales promotion.

左／1895年に建築家 Henry Ives Cobb が設計したオランダ様式の建物は現在シカゴにこの一軒のみ残っている
その由緒ある建物をレストランに変えた
右／横の道路にも大きなサインを配している

33 West Kinzie Chicago, Illinois 60610
Phone/312-465-9269

Left, bottom / At present, there is only one Dutch style building in Chicago. This time-honored
    building designed in 1895 by the architect Henry Ives Cobb, was redecorated into a restaurant.
Right, bottom / There is a large sign placed by the side road.

50フィートの長いカウンターを設け　ランチタイムにはロースト＆コーンドビーフ　サンドイッチを提供するカービング　ステーションを置く
The long (50 feet) counter. At lunch time, a curbing station is placed to offer roasted & corned beef sandwiches.

ハリー カリーズ

シカゴではスポーツ界で活躍した選手やアナウ
ンサー達が開業したレストランが話題になって
いる。"シカゴベアーズ"のコーチだったマイク
ディトカが「Ditka's」を同じチームのクォータ
ーバックだったジム マックマホンが「Jim Mc-
Mahon's」(本書68ページ収録)というぐあい
である。そして"シカゴカブス"の名アナウン
サーだったハリー カリーがこのレストランのパ
ートナーオーナーとなっているが いずれも連
日にぎわっている。3店ともこの2年以内にオ
ープンしたもので スポーツファンを中心とし
た客層をつかんでいる。
1985年に建てられたオランダ様式の建物を生か
し 野球に関する数々のすばらしい想い出を表
現するコレクションを店内に飾り アメリカン
・イタリアン料理を提供するレストランとサロ
ンといった感じの店である。
開店／1987年10月23日
営業時間／11:30AM～ 2:00PM(ランチ：月～金)
　　　　　5:30AM～10:00PM(ディナー：日～木)
　　　　　5:30PM～12:00AM(ディナー：金・土)
客席数／175席

HARRY CARAY'S

In Chicago, restaurants opened by sportsmen
and announcers who were active in the sports
world, are becoming popular. "Ditka's" has
been opened by Mike Ditka, a former coach of
the "Chicago Bears," while "Jim McMahon's"
(that appears on page 68 of this book) has
been established by Jim McMahon who played as a quarterback of the same team.
Harry Caray, a former star announcer for the
"Chicago Cabs" is a co-owner of this "Harry
Caray's" that is prospering everyday.
These three restaurants opened during the
past two years, with many sports fans as
their main guests.
In the Dutch style building constructed in
1985, a collection of pieces that recall various
wonderful baseball events is displayed, and
American-Italian dishes are served – a restaurant with an atmosphere of salon.

Opened / October 23, 1987
Open /　11:30 a.m. to 2:00 p.m.
　　　　　　(lunch: Monday to Friday)
　　　　　5:30 a.m. to 10:00 p.m.
　　　　　　(dinner: Sunday to Thursday)
　　　　　5:30 p.m. to 12:00 a.m.
　　　　　　(dinner: Friday · Saturday)
No. of guest seats /175

バーカウンターにはマホガニー材を用い　1890年代のレストランを表現する窓や天井デザインも再現している

オリジナルのテラッゾーフロアを再現した店内とサービスステーションのコーナー
The inside where the original terrazzo floor is reproduced, and the corner for service station.

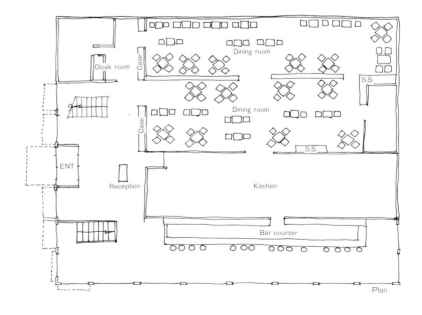

Left / The bar counter uses mahogany, while the window and ceiling are arranged to give an image of restaurant in the 1890's.

上／スペシャル ポークチョップ イタリアンスタイル
下／イタリアの火山を表現したチキン料理 Chicken Vesuvio

Top / Special pork chop Italian style.
Bottom / Chicken Vesuvio — expressing the Italian volcano.

上／球界の歴史や博物館などに置くべき記念物が収集され　飾られ
ているダイニングルームは２つの部屋に分けられている
左／野球に関する数々の素晴しい想い出のコレクションを飾るダイ
ニングルーム

Top / Divided into two rooms, the dining room is decorated
　　　with a collection of various mementoes telling the history
　　　of baseball that should be kept at a museum, etc.
Left / The dining room where a wonderful collection of
　　　various mementoes about baseball are displayed.

上／レセプション近くよりダイニングエリアを結ぶ階段廻りをみる　イタリアに関する情報を壁面に掲示している
　モザイク状のフロアがユニーク
下／上段のテーブル席よりオープンキッチン方向をみる

Top / The staircase area connecting the dining area viewed from a place near the reception. Information about Italy is given on the wall. The mosaic floor is unique.
Bottom / The open kitchen area viewed from the upper stage table seats.

410 West Huron Chicago, Illinois 60610
Phone／312-943-5900

レセプションよりバーコーナーをみる　ボトルを飾っている明るい窓はガレージ入口の扉があった位置　当店自慢の女性用トイレの入口がみえる
The bar corner viewed from the reception.　At the place where there is a bright window with bottles displayed, was a door of the garage's entrance. The entrance to women's toilet — the pride of this restaurant — is visible.

レセプションよりバーコーナー　ダイニングエリアをみる　アーチ状の梁　モザイク状のフロア　オールド イタリアンの雰囲気を出した壁面が特徴

The bar corner and dining area viewed from the reception. The arched beams, mosaic floor and wall surface giving an old Italian atmosphere.

オープンキッチンの横に設けたテーブルクロス用の白いロールペーパー　　　　The white roll paper for tablecloth provided beside the open kitchen.

スクージ

シカゴのレストラン経営者 Richard Melman 氏を中心に　現在注目を浴びている「レタス エンターティン ユー社(Lettuce Entertain You)」が「Ed Devevic's」や「Cafe Ba-Ba-Reeba」に続き1986年幕に開店した　北イタリアの田舎風レストランをテーマに新しいコンセプトを打ち出して成功している店である。

ダウンタウンに隣接する倉庫街の一角にあったガレージを改装したもので　内装はすべて新しい造りであるがオールド イタリアンの雰囲気を出すために意識的に古く見せている。壁面には　薄く剥がれた部分をつくり　その下から煉瓦のブリックが現れている。325席の広大な店内は　アーチ状の天井に木を使った梁を幾つか設け　中央部分には一本の柱も使用しないという見事な演出である。また女性用のトイレは4〜5部屋に分けられ　それぞれの部屋の演出も異なり話題づくりに一役買っている。連日ディナーのみの営業だが　電話での予約は一切受け付けず　店での待ち時間は平均1時間半という超繁盛店である。客層は若い専門職や女性の姿も非常に多く見られる。

開店／1986年12月22日
営業時間／5:00PM〜10:30PM(ディナー：月〜木)
　　　　　5:00PM〜11:30PM(ディナー：金・土)
　　　　　4:00PM〜 9:00PM(ディナー：日)
客席数／325席　従業員数／150人

SCOOZI

Opened at the end of 1986 by "Lettuce Entertain You" under the leadership of Richard Melman, restaurant operator in Chicago, "Scoozi" has introduced successfully the image of a rustic restaurant of North Italy. Lettuce Entertain You has already opened "Ed Devevic's" and "Café Ba-Ba-Reeba."

This restaurant has been constructed by redecorating a garage at a corner of a warehouse street adjacent to downtown. Though the interior is totally new, its finish gives deliberately an look old to it to produce an old Italian atmosphere. The wall has parts that have come off, and the inner brick surface is exposed. The wide internal space with 325 seats is designed wonderfully with the arched ceiling with several wooden beams, using no pillars in the central area. Toilets for women are divided into 4 to 5 rooms, each with different presentation – another feature of this restaurant.

Operated only for dinner, this restaurant does not accept any reservation by phone, and guests must usually wait for about an hour and a half for their turn. A prosperous and popular restaurant frequented by many young professionals and ladies.

Opened / December 22, 1986
Open /　5:00 p.m. to 10:30 p.m. (dinner: Monday to Thursday)
　　　　5:00 p.m. to 11:30 p.m. (dinner: Friday · Saturday)
　　　　4:00 p.m. to 9:00 p.m. (dinner: Sunday)
No. of guest seats / 325
No. of employees / 150

ダイニングエリアにはアーチ状の梁を設け広いスペースなのに柱がみえない
The arched beams used for the dining area — the beams are out of sight despite the wide space.

個性を演出した女性用トイレ
The women's toilet with individualistic presentation.

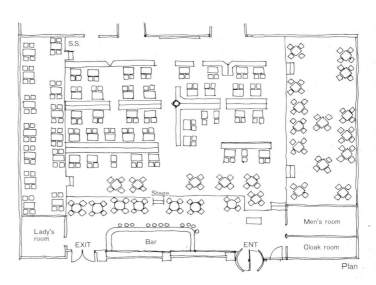

Plan

EXIT

段差を付けたダイニングエリアよりバーコーナーをみる

The bar corner viewed from the dining area differing in level.

当店自慢の大きなピザ Spaccata　　　　　　　　The large pizza spaccata — the pride of this restaurant.

ファサード　入口上方に大きなトマトを吊げたユニークな演出
The facade with unique presentation of a large tomato suspended from an upper part of the entrance.

通りに面したアウトドア ポーチは夏期のみ開放され　カクテルと軽い食事が楽しめる
The outdoor porch facing the street is opened in summer alone, where guests can enjoy cocktail and light meal.

GoRdoN
Aioli, Smoked Bell

500 North Clark St. Chicago, Illinois 60610
Phone/312-467-9780

ファサード　　　　　　　　　　　　　　　　　The facade.

入口を入ったレセプションあたり　ピアノも置かれ　数々の賞や有名人たちのサインや写真などがその上に置かれている
Around the reception beside the entrance. On the piano are placed various prizes, signatures and photos of celebrity, etc.

ゴードン

健康や栄養についての考え方が国民の間で一段と強く叫ばれているアメリカでは　レストランの料理においても同様な配慮がなされてきている。軽くスチームした野菜や塩分などの少ない味つけ　クリームをできるだけ使用しないで　野菜のピューレを使うソース マリネや酢を用いた調理法などが新しいアメリカの料理として人気を得てきている。

ゴードン シンクレア (Gordon Sinclir) 氏は12年前に彼の店を持った時から健康と栄養　美しい皿の盛りつけをモットーにしている。さらに最近移転した店内はローマの郊外の劇場を模したインテリアで　インフォーマルななかにエレガントな雰囲気を造り出し人気を得ている。このような彼の姿勢は多くの人たちに認められ　業界No.1の「Restaurants & Instituions」誌の"アイビー賞"を1986年に与えられ　名誉あるレストラン経営者の一人に加わった。

開店／1984年12月15日
営業時間／11:30AM〜 2:30PM（ランチ：火〜金）
　　　　　　　　5:30PM〜10:30PM（ディナー）
休日／なし
客席数／140席
従業員数／60人
客単価／ランチ28ドル　ディナー35ドル

GORDON

In the U.S. where people are becoming more conscious of health and diet, similar considerations have been given to the nature of restaurant dishes, such as lightly steamed vegetables, seasoning with less salt, sauce marinier using vegetable purée with a minimum of cream, cooking that uses vinegar, etc. These items are becoming popular as new-type American dishes.

Since he opened his restaurant 12 years ago, Gordon Sinclair has clung to health, diet and beautiful dishing up as his motto. Recently he has moved his restaurant to this place. The interior gives the image of a theater in the suburbs of Rome, and the restaurant has gained popularity by featuring an informal, elegant atmosphere. The policy of this owner has been welcomed by many people, and in 1986 he was awarded with the "Ivy Prize" by the trade's No. 1 "Restaurants & Institutions" magazine, to become one of the honorable restaurant operators.

Opened / December 15, 1984
Open / 11:30 a.m. to 2:30 p.m. (lunch: Tuesday to Friday)
　　　　 5:30 p.m. to 10:30 p.m. (dinner)
Closed / None
No. of guest seats / 140
No. of employees / 60
Price per guest / lunch: $28,　dinner: $35

手前のテーブル席と一段高くなった奥の壁面のある席は　ローマ風シアターの雰囲気が感じられる
The front table seat area, and inner seat area by the wall that is a little higher than the surrounding area, have an atmosphere of Roman theater.

シカゴの女性アーチストの作品による壁面構成は　このレストランの自慢のひとつ
The wall composition of a Chicagoan female artist's works is another pride of this restaurant.

ローマ郊外の劇場を模したインテリアは　インフォーマルななかにエレガントな雰囲気をもっている
The interior modeled after that of a theater in the suburbs of Rome, has an informal, but elegant atmosphere.

ティファニーランプや季節の花々がテーブル席に飾られ　スタイリッシュなレストランとして評価されている
Tiffany lamp and season's flowers are set on each table, helping this restaurant to be recognized as being stylish.

218

セラミックタイル ローズウッド ラタン マーブルといった材質がふんだんに使用されているダイニングルーム
Materials, such as ceramic tiles, rosewood, latten and marble, are abundantly used.

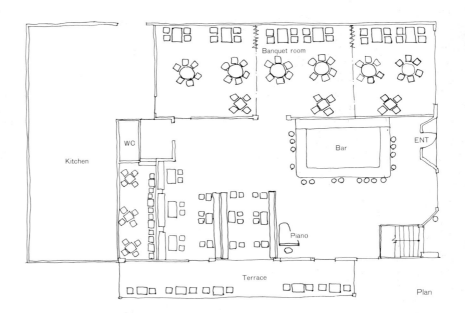

Plan

11席のバーコーナーの雰囲気も重厚で　ハードリカーの他にワインのコレクションも多い
The bar corner with 11 seats also has a dignified atmosphere, featuring a rich collection of hard liquor and wine.

1／自家製スモークサーモン
2／グリルド サーモンの中国マスタード塗り
3／ソフトシェルクラブのソテー
4／ゴードンデザート プラッター（２人前）

The main dishes.

ファサード　コミュニティS.C.内の出店て駐車場は共有して利用
The facade. Opened within the Community S.C., the parking lot is used in common.

サインボード　S.C.内の出店やフリースタンディングのユニットなど立地も多様
The signboard, opening within the S.C., free-standing unit — a variety
of arrangements.

1906 Lincoln Blvd. Santa Monica, CA 90405
Phone/213-392-9809

オーダーカウンターをみる　カウボーイハットをかぶった若い従業員が客を迎えてくれる　　The order counter. The cowboy-hatted young staff welcomes you.

オーダーカウンター越しに見せる大きな炭焼きグリルとマリネのチキン
The large charcoal grill and marinated chicken that can be seen across the order counter.

オープングリルの見えるオーダーカウンターあたり

The order counter area that is visible at the open grill.

ポピュラーなアイテムは3ピースのチキンコンボ　スパニッシュライス　ビーンズ　サルサとフラワートルテーヤ付き
The popular item is three pieces of chicken compote, with Spanish rice, beans, sarsa and flower tortilla.

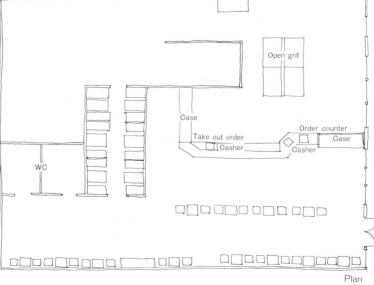

Open grill

Case

Take out order

Order counter

Casher

Case

Casher

WC

Plan

エル ポヨ ロコ

コーヒーショップのデニーズ社が展開するメキ
シカン スタイルのチキンを主力商品としたチェ
ーン店である。大きなチャコールを燃やすグリ
ルをオープンキッチンに設け フルーツジュー
スとスパイス類とハーブなどに漬け込んでマリ
ネしたチキンをカウボーイハットをかぶった従
業員が焼いているが その演出がいい。これは
1975年にメキシコで生まれたコンセプトを取り
入れたものである。
最近の健康志向にそって なるべく油を使用し
ない料理が人気を得ているが この店の調理法
はその意図にそったものといえるだろう。そし
て"米国心臓病協会"の推奨する脂肪分コレスト
ロールなどの基準に適合するものとして セー
ルスプロモーションにも大いに力を注いでい
る。1988年3月現在 南カリフォルニア地域におけ
る出店数は準備中も含めて108店舗となってい
る。
営業時間／10：00AM〜10：00PM

EL POLLO LOCO

This is restaurant in the mainly Mexican-style
chicken food chain that has been being developed by Dennies, a coffee shop chain.
With a grill burning large charcoal in the open
kitchen, cowboy hatted staffs are roasting
chicken marinated in fruit juice, spices, herbs,
etc., presenting a nice cooking scene. This
concept was born in 1975 in Mexico.
Reflecting the recent health-conscious trends,
dishes that use less oil are gaining in popularity. The cooking method at this restaurant
is said to be following these trends. The
operator is also endeavoring towards sales
promotion by stressing that these foods com-
ply with standards for fats, cholesterol, etc.
as recommended by the American Heart
Disease Association. As of March 1988, the
number of shops that are already open and
will be opened in South California totals 108.

Open / 10:00 a.m. to 10:00 p.m.

客席は4人用と2人用のブースで テーマカラーの赤色が椅子やテーブルトップのアクセントとなっている

店内の奥より店頭をみる　サービスエリアにベビー用の椅子もある
The shop-front viewed from an inner part of the shop. Baby chairs are also available at the service area.

メニュー
The menu.

Left / The guest seat area consists of booths for four and two guests, accented with the theme color on chairs, tabletop, etc.

シカゴのダウンタウンにあるリバーノース地区に出店したレストランの外観
The appearance of the restaurant opened at River North District in downtown Chicago.

358 West Ontario Chicago, Illinois 60610
Phone/312-440-4900

レセプション近くに設けたミートのショーケース
The meat showcase installed near the reception.

228

100席のフルサービスバー

The full-service bar with 100 seats.

田舎風のカジュアル エレガンスのダイニングエリア 奥にチャコールピットが見える
The dining area featuring a rustic, casual elegance. The charcoal pits are visible at an inner part.

レセプションと一段明るいミートのショーケースを備えたコーナーをみる
The reception and the corner with a brighter meat showcase.

ザ ブッチャー ショップ

ヘルシィフードが流行のアメリカでステーキハウスの紹介とは？ と感じられるかも知れないが 今またステーキの売上げが伸びてきている。米国民が長く慣れ親しんだステーキが そう簡単に忘れ去られるものではないという証明でもあるようだ。このレストランはテネシー州メンフィスに1981年に1号店を開店し 最も新しいシカゴ店は5店目にあたる。この店のユニークなコンセプトはフィレミニオン トップサーロインなど5種類の肉をそれぞれ異なる重さで提供し 価格15.15ドルに統一している。そして客に自ら備えつけの3つの大きなチャコールピットで好みに合わせて焼いてもらうというのが狙いだ。但し 当店のシェフに焼いてもらうと2ドルの追加になる。コンベンションなどの多いシカゴでグループでバーベキューを楽しめるというので好評である。

開店／1987年10月10日
営業時間／11:30AM～ 2:30PM（ランチ：月～金）
　　　　　 5:30PM～10:30PM（ディナー）
従業員数／70～80人
客単価／25ドル

230

数多いボトルのコレクションが自慢のバーカウンター

The bar counter featuring a collection of many bottles.

THE BUTCHER SHOP

One might wonder why I introduce a steak house in the current America where health foods are popular. Now, again, steak sales are increasing. This seems to prove that steak, to which Americans have been accustomed for a long time, cannot be forgotton so easily. This Chicago shop is the fifth in the chain, since the first shop was opened in 1981 in Memphis, Mississippi. The unique concept of this shop is that any of five types of meat (fillet minion, top sirloin, etc.) is served with a different weight but for a fixed price of $15.15, and that guests are asked to roast at any of the three charcoal pits according to their own taste. If they ask the chef to roast for them, then an additional $2 will be charged. In Chicago where conventions, etc. are often held, this shop is frequented by groups of guests who like to enjoy barbecue.

Opened / October 10, 1987
Open / 11:30 a.m. to 2:30 p.m. (lunch: Monday to Friday)
          5:30 p.m. to 10:30 p.m. (dinner)
No. of employees / 70 to 80
Price per guest / $25

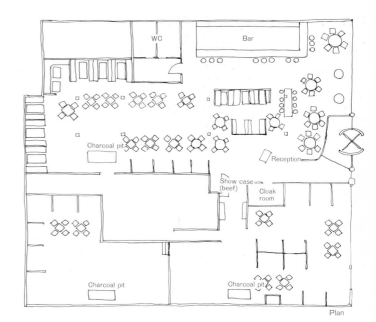

Plan

カジュアルな雰囲気て田舎風造りのダイニングエリア

The casual dining area of rustic makeup.

シカゴをテーマにしたビルや風景の親しみある絵をたくさん飾っている
Many pictures of familiar buildings and scenes of Chicago.

練瓦で造った大きなチャコールピットは　３つの部屋のダイニングエリアにそれぞれ備えて
ある
The large bricked charcoal pit is set in the dining area of each of three rooms.

格調のある鉄製の扉があるレストランのファサード

The facade of the restaurant with a dignified iron door.

CAMELIONS

246 26th St. Santa Monica, CA 9002
Phone/213-395-0746

女性オーナーの意図を強く反映しているのか 店内は家族的な雰囲気の中にエレガントさを感じる
Probably reflecting the female owner's intention, the inside gives an elegant impression in the homely atmosphere.

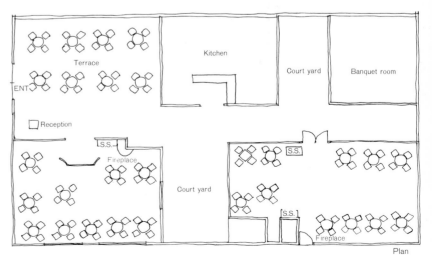

Plan

後方にあるパティオとダイニングルームはレセプションにも開放している
The patio and dining room at the back are also opened as a reception.

オープンエアのテラス席が中庭に設けてあり ランチタイムには人気がある
The open-air terrace seats are installed in the courtyard, and popular at lunch time.

後方にあるもうひとつの部屋もダイニングルームとして使用し　他にテラス席とプライベートルームがある
This room at the back is also used as a dining room.　A terrace seat area and a private room are also provided.

暖炉を配した後方のダイニングルーム

The backward dining room provided with a fireplace.

カメリオンズ

店名は中世の英語で　現在のカメレオン（Chameleon）と同意語であるが　それはメニューがよく変わり　その時々に応じた適切な対応をしていくレストランという意味を含めて女性オーナーのマーシャ　サンズさんが名づけたという。このレストランのシェフは若干26歳の女性であるが　12歳の時にはレストランで皿洗いをしていたという程料理に関心を持ち　今では彼女の努力と才能が多くの料理批評家などにも高く評価されている。

サンタモニカの高級住宅地に立地し　カリフォルニア産の素材を活かしたフランス料理を提供している。建築はジョン　バイヤーズ氏が手掛けたもので　築後60年といわれるスペイン調の邸宅をレストランに改装　開店したもので話題を呼んでいる。

営業時間／11：30AM〜　2：00PM（ランチ：火〜土）
　　　　　　6：00PM〜11：00PM（ディナー：火〜土）
　　　　　　11：00AM〜　2：00PM（ブランチ：日）
　　　　　　5：00PM〜10：00PM（ディナー：日）
客席数／49席（メインダイニング）　100席（テラス　＆　プライベートルーム）
従業員数／40人
客単価／ランチ 15〜16ドル　ディナー 30〜35ドル

CAMELIONS

"Camelion" is a medieval English word meaning "chameleon," and this restaurant name has been adopted by the owner Marsha Sans to imply that her menu changes from time to time, and offer seasonable dishes. The chef who is a young lady (26 years old) was so interested in cooking that she had even worked as a dish-washer in a restaurant when she was 12 years old. Now, her efforts and talent are highly recognized by many cooking critics. Situated at a high-class residential quarter in Santa Monica, "Camelions" is offering French dishes that use Californian materials. The construction has been undertaken by John Buyers who redecorated the 60 year-old Spanish residence into a restaurant. Since its opening, it has been highly rated.

Open /　11:30 a.m. to 2:00 p.m. (lunch: Tuesday to Saturday)
　　　　　6:00 p.m. to 11:00 p.m. (dinner: Tuesday to Saturday)
　　　　　11:00 a.m. to 2:00 p.m. (brunch: Sunday)
　　　　　5:00 p.m. to 10:00 p.m. (dinner: Sunday)
No. of guest seats / 49 (main dining), 100 (terrace & private room)
No. of employees / 40
Price per guest / lunch: $15 to 16, dinner: $30 to 35

パティオよりスペイン調の邸宅を改装したメインダイニングルームと続く入口
The entrance. Leading from the patio to the main dining brought into being by redecorating the Spanish residence.

① ② ③

1／鮪のカルパチオ　アボカド添え
2／カリフォルニア産養殖すずきのソテー　トマトとバジルの"コリンス"ソース
3／仔牛のチョップロースト モレルとセロリーの根の薄切り　マッシュルーム添え　オニオンとローズマリーのマーマレードソース

The main dishes.